The Genealogy of Modern Feminist Thinking

Within much contemporary feminist theory there is a tendency to forget or ignore its own historicity and consider itself as primarily oriented towards the present. This book explores the historical roots of some of feminism's central concepts and debates, examining the philosophical conditions for feminist thought and taking as its point of departure the dynamic relationship between feminist thought and the history of philosophy. With close attention to the genealogy of key concepts such as equality, sex/gender and difference, alongside discussions of contemporary gender equality policy and contextual understandings of central figures including Wollstonecraft, Beauvoir and Irigaray, *The Genealogy of Modern Feminist Thinking* provides an analysis of feminism from its origins in the Early Modern period to its contemporary, post-modern forms. Shedding light on feminism as a product of Modernity and establishing it as part of the canon of European intellectual development, this book thus corrects the picture of feminism as a phenomenon that lacks historical continuity, revealing a history characterized by breaks, setbacks and forgetting, in which the forgetting itself forms part of a rich genealogy. As such, it will be of interest to philosophers, sociologists, political theorists and intellectual historians alike.

Ingeborg W. Owesen is Senior Adviser and Coordinator for the Research Council of Norway and co-author of *The History of Gender Equality in Norway 1814–2013*. She holds a PhD in philosophy.

Routledge Research in Gender and Society

The Gender-Sensitive University
A Contradiction in Terms?
Edited by Eileen Drew and Siobhan Canavan

Trauma Transmission and Sexual Violence
Reconciliation and Peacebuilding in Post-Conflict Settings
Nena Močnik

Men, Masculinities and Intimate Partner Violence
Edited by Lucas Gottzén, Margunn Bjørnholt, and Floretta Boonzaier

Political Invisibility and Mobilization
Women against State Violence in Argentina, Yugoslavia, and Liberia
Selina Gallo-Cruz

Multiple Gender Cultures, Sociology, and Plural Modernities
Re-reading Social Constructions of Gender across the Globe in a Decolonial Perspective
Edited by Heidemarie Winkel and Angelika Poferl

Women of Faith and the Quest for Spiritual Authenticity
Comparative Perspectives from Malaysia and Britain
Sara Ashencaen Crabtree

The Genealogy of Modern Feminist Thinking
Feminist Thought as Historical Present
Ingeborg W. Owesen

For more information about this series, please visit:
https://www.routledge.com/Routledge-Research-in-Gender-and-Society/book-series/SE0271

The Genealogy of Modern Feminist Thinking
Feminist Thought as Historical Present

Ingeborg W. Owesen

LONDON AND NEW YORK

First published 2021
by Routledge
2 Park Square, Milton Park, Abingdon, Oxon OX14 4RN

and by Routledge
605 Third Avenue, New York, NY 10158

Routledge is an imprint of the Taylor & Francis Group, an informa business

© 2021 Ingeborg W. Owesen

The right of Ingeborg W. Owesen to be identified as author of this work has been asserted by her in accordance with sections 77 and 78 of the Copyright, Designs and Patents Act 1988.

All rights reserved. No part of this book may be reprinted or reproduced or utilised in any form or by any electronic, mechanical, or other means, now known or hereafter invented, including photocopying and recording, or in any information storage or retrieval system, without permission in writing from the publishers.

Trademark notice: Product or corporate names may be trademarks or registered trademarks, and are used only for identification and explanation without intent to infringe.

The author has received funding from the Norwegian Non-Fiction Writers Association and the Fritt Ord Foundation.

British Library Cataloguing-in-Publication Data
A catalogue record for this book is available from the British Library

Library of Congress Cataloging-in-Publication Data
A catalog record has been requested for this book

ISBN: 978-0-367-68171-5 (hbk)
ISBN: 978-0-367-68172-2 (pbk)
ISBN: 978-1-003-13451-0 (ebk)

Typeset in Times New Roman
by Taylor & Francis Books

Contents

	Acknowledgements	vi
	Introduction	1
1	Feminism as a modern phenomenon	11
2	Philosophies of equality	24
3	Cartesian feminism	44
4	Citizenship, education and the vote	61
5	The difference that makes a difference	79
	Concluding remarks	92
	Bibliography	93
	Index	99

Acknowledgements

I owe debts of gratitude to several people and have more intellectual debts than I can easily name. This book has had a long creation. It first began as an idea built upon a postdoctoral project at the Centre for Women's Studies and Gender Research at the University of Oslo in 2012. The chapters have been written on and off over a period of eight years, leaving thoughts to develop and change.

I have been granted financial support from the Research Council of Norway, the Norwegian Non-Fiction Writers and Translators Association, Solveig Wexelsen Eriksen's Trust and the Fritt Ord Foundation. I was also lucky to be offered a place as a visiting scholar at the National Library in Oslo for one semester. Without support from these sources, this project would not have seen the light of day.

I would especially like to thank the following colleagues for constructive and insightful comments: Hilde Bondevik, Helene Aarseth, Kari Solbrække, Lise Christensen and Tove Pettersen. My dear son and colleague Erlend W. F. Owesen read through and commented on every single chapter.

Finally, I thank my friends and family for their patience, support and sympathy, particularly both my children, Erlend and Ida. The book is dedicated to the memory of my father, Albert W. Owesen.

Introduction

Historical consciousness

This book sets out to uncover the philosophical background for feminist thought. Contemporary feminism builds upon a tradition that has only recently begun to be explored. The ambition of this book is to fill a gap in the history of feminism and the history of philosophy by turning feminism into its own object of analysis. To this end, I aim to reveal some of the philosophical origins of key concepts within feminist thought, such as equality, gender as a cultural construction, citizenship, the divide between sex and gender, etc. I wish not only to show the history of feminist thought and its relevance for contemporary feminist thinking, but also to bring feminist voices from the past and the present into a dialogue.

Contemporary feminist theory is largely oriented towards the present. This book aims at looking seriously at the historical intellectual background and history of modern feminism (also often referred to as first and second wave), and some of its contemporary debates. The book is a study of the philosophical conditions for feminist thought without necessarily constructing a progressive linear perspective, but rather presenting a genealogy, so to speak. Genealogy being a historical account, tracking the lineage of a concept and revealing its origin. The philosophical history of modern feminism is for many still an unknown territory. This history might reveal itself as a valuable source for contemporary feminism in as much as there are several parallels between the arguments of the past and those of present. There has been relatively little explicit or systematic attention in recent years to the questioning of the intellectual roots of modern feminism. This seems to be a neglected area within feminist literature, but an area in which there is a huge potential for interdisciplinary research as well as philosophical research.

2 Introduction

The intention of the book is to follow the development of the philosophical arguments for the development of an autonomous, secular feminist discourse and particularly to show the importance of Early Modern Cartesianism. There is a dynamic relationship between feminist thought and the history of philosophy. My aim is to offer a twofold gain as feminism will be approached from a philosophical historical perspective, while at the same time the history of philosophy will be approached from a feminist perspective. Thus the ultimate purpose or goal of such a historiography of feminism is to incorporate feminist thinking into the canon of European intellectual history. Feminism is not something in the margins of European culture, but right at the heart of it.

This book differs from other studies of historical dimensions of feminism by its philosophical objectives. Feminism can be distinguished as (a) a social and political movement and (b) a set of ideas. The existing literature on the history of feminism is for the most part written by historians who treat feminism primarily as a socio-political movement (e.g. Rendall, 1985, Cott, 1987, Scott, 1996, Offen, 2000). My account differs from these by its identification of feminism as a set of ideas. Feminist philosophers, on the other hand, who *do* study ideas, tend to focus on individual thinkers, concepts or topics isolated from historical background. The fact that feminism existed prior to Women's Lib and the 1970s is often overlooked (e.g. Irigaray, 1985, Butler, 1990, Grosz, 1994). This study aims at bringing historical consciousness and post-structuralist theories and contemporary feminism together. One way of addressing this is by the term "historical present". Within feminist philosophy, feminism often figures as a perspective upon something else, while this book wants to turn feminism itself into an object of (feminist) study and analysis.

The historical line will be drawn from Early Modernity to Post-Modernity, from Descartes and Marie de Gournay and up until contemporary feminist thinking and debates. Approaching feminism as a set of ideas also has the benefit of letting us locate isolated or forgotten feminists whose work was poorly understood or neglected during their time. The last decades of feminist research has re-discovered several "forgotten" thinkers and made many of their texts available by new publications and translations (e.g. University of Chicago Press's series "The Other Voice in Early Modern Europe"). Owing gratitude to these re-discoveries, it is now possible to reconstruct a genealogy or history of feminism.

The book will as mentioned focus around central concepts within feminist thought. The history, or genealogy, of feminist thinking can be viewed as a history of these concepts. It must also be said that the book at hand is not an introduction to feminist theory or thinking. The text presupposes knowledge of the field and will e.g. speak of Simone de Beauvoir and Mary Wollstonecraft and others as if the reader is already somewhat familiar with these thinkers. Covering such a large span in history, however, it is necessary to compensate for this general and universal outlook with some chosen close readings and a selection of the most significant names in the history of feminism will figure as protagonists through several chapters. Sometimes they will also be brought into conversation with each other.

What I by way of introduction described as a tendency to be primarily oriented towards the present and ignore history and the past is not only a feature of feminism; philosophy also struggles with related problems. Charles Taylor's description of philosophy's relation to its history seems to have many points of resemblance with feminism's relation to *its* history:

> There is an ideal, a goal that surfaces from time to time in philosophy. The inspiration to sweep away the past and have an understanding of things which is entirely contemporary. The attractive idea underlying this is that of liberation from the dead weight of past errors and illusions. Thought cast off its chains.
> (Taylor, 1984: 17)

The ambition of this project, however, is to tie threads together and establish connections between contemporary feminist theory and the history of feminism.

Feminist thinking has developed in parallel and constant dialogue with the history of philosophy. Feminism is inspired and influenced by philosophical positions, e.g. rationalism, empiricism and liberalism are all philosophical positions that stimulate equality between the sexes. Both male and female feminist theorists imported and transformed the most radical thoughts and ideas of their own present into a feminist connection. A substantial part of this book is invested in tracking these philosophical positions and the feminist interpretation of them. To give an example; François Poulain de la Barre (1647–1732) re-wrote Descartes with a feminist objective. Poulain applied Cartesian principles to "the Woman Question" and demonstrated by a "rational deduction" that the supposedly self-evident inequality of the sexes was nothing more than unfounded prejudice. Poulain argued that women's "natural" inferiority was culturally produced, an argument that has a great similarity with Simone de Beauvoir's main thesis that "one is not born, but rather becomes woman". One can even say that Poulain anticipates 20th century feminism's sex/gender divide.

The book will also argue that historical consciousness is crucial for feminism, for several reasons. One reason is that without historical knowledge or cultural memory we risk having to "invent the wheel" all over again. Gender as a cultural construction is often thought of as a radical and new idea, but in fact similar ideas were proposed by feminists of the 16th and 17th centuries. Historical consciousness is also important in order to understand that feminism is a process, and a process that is still going on. I will still abstain from constructing feminism as a teleological story of cumulative progress toward an ever-elusive goal. The history of feminism is equally marked by repetitions, forgetting and backlash as theory development and breakthrough. Thus, the method of genealogy, as developed by Nietzsche in *Genealogy of Morals,* and continued by Michel Foucault, lends a useful tool. A genealogical method will be combined with *Geistesgeschichte* (intellectual history), which according to Richard Rorty is a synthesis between "historical reconstruction" and "rational reconstruction" (Rorty, 1984).

The historical framework of the book is constituted by Early Modernity at one end and contemporary feminist theory at the other. One of the ambitions is to challenge the picture of feminism as a phenomenon that lacks historical continuity. Feminism *does* have a history, a history that is often ignored and forgotten, paradoxically even by feminists and genderstudies scholars. Feminism has a history albeit one characterized by breaks, setbacks and forgetting, of which the forgetting of its own history is part of the genealogy.

The chapters will be organized around central concepts and topics within feminist thinking. These are for example the concept of equality, gender as a cultural construction, the importance of education and vote, and otherness and difference. This will also allow for a contextualization of some of feminism's most prominent thinkers and will for example counter the widespread portrayal of Mary Wollstonecraft as an isolated pioneer. Contextualization will place Wollstonecraft in her philosophical environment and present. Wollstonecraft was a radical political thinker fighting for political reform regarding women's access to citizenship, education, marital status, women's right to property, inheritance, parental rights to their own children as well as the abolishment of slavery, to mention a few of the cases she was involved in. Wollstonecraft's thoughts were not developed in a vacuum but were shaped by the thoughts and discussions of her own time. She was for example strongly influenced by John Locke's ideas on upbringing and education. She was also familiar with the works of Edmund Burke, Thomas Paine, David Hume and Adam Smith. Translating and reviewing Enlightenment literature made her conversant with not just

Introduction 5

English, but also German and French thinking such as that of Voltaire, Rousseau, Kant and Leibniz. This book will try to analyze how Wollstonecraft imports the philosophical impulses of her own present and applies them into a feminist agenda. Wollstonecraft's actuality is also manifested in her anticipation of the later Simone de Beauvoir's principal idea that woman is made into man's other. Wollstonecraft blames women's imperative to please men as the source for their being always a part of man. Re-written into Beauvoirian terms, woman is thus never being-in-herself, but always being-for-an-other, for man. (More on Wollstonecraft in Chapter 4.)

The relationship between feminism and mainstream philosophy is also a two-way dynamic relationship. As we shall see in the example of Marie de Gournay, feminism was ahead of mainstream thinking in the case of equality.

Restoring the past – a third way

The approach in this book is to see the tradition, i.e. the history of philosophy as a source rather than an object of criticism. Early feminist history of philosophy focused on (a) historical exclusion of female philosophers and (b) what canonical philosophers had to say about women. This attitude led to e.g. interpretations of reason and objectivity as male (Lloyd, 1984, Bordo, 1987, Okin, 1979). Feminist philosophers have criticized both the historical exclusion of women *from* the philosophical tradition, and the negative characterization of the feminine *in* it. While feminist philosophers usually have focused on either of these two criticisms, my perspective here is different: to read the canon of philosophy as an accomplice and source rather than an enemy and target. I will argue that the modern canon of philosophy can be read as a condition of possibility for feminism and liberation of women altogether.

We can distinguish between a *negative* and *positive* approach to the canon. While a negative relation includes approaches that focus on the misogyny of a philosopher or on gendered interpretations of specific concepts, a positive relation emphasizes how feminists inherit resources from the tradition that are productive for contemporary feminist concerns.[1] One could perhaps say that feminism in academia is a fairly recent phenomenon and that the overall negative attitude belongs to its "childhood". A more positive appropriation of the philosophical tradition is also pointed out by Genevieve Lloyd:

> The positive and negative approaches can both be seen as reflecting a feminist perspective on the history of philosophy, but they're

6 *Introduction*

very different in spirit. I'm now much more interested in the positive appropriations – in looking to sources in the philosophical tradition for ways of reconceptualising issues that are under current debate, and for ways of thinking, than I am in the more negative criticisms of past philosophers.

(Lloyd, 2000: 45)

Lloyd also admits that in *The Man of Reason* (1984) she was looking at the more negative points of the philosophical tradition but that, if she were to look at Descartes now, she would do it very differently. (See further discussion on interpretations of Descartes in Chapter 3.) My point is simply to place this project in a more recent positive attitude towards the tradition. What the earlier critical approach *did* manage to put on the map, however, is that gender *is* a category to analyze history from. Gender matters and has been a focus for philosophers throughout history. Questions of gender have thus not been excluded from the canon, but what has been excluded is the history of feminism, i.e. the history of how gender equality came about. To map out this history we don't need to fight fire with fire but to see that the tradition is on our side. It is a source that can be productive for contemporary feminist concerns.

The negative feminist approach does not only take place within philosophy. Other examples include historian Joan Kelly, who claimed that women did not have a Renaissance, that they did not have a share in this golden age of human civilization (Kelly, 1984). In Kelly's interpretation the period was one of decline for women where elite women lost power and autonomy. A more recent historical study by Cissie Fairchilds contends that this is not the case (Fairchild, 2007). Fairchilds emphasizes the positive changes in the lives of women in the same period and claims that the patriarchal paradigm was increasingly challenged by intellectuals, both male and female. Joan Scott's groundbreaking work *Only Paradoxes to Offer* suggests by its title that early European feminism had little more than paradoxes to offer (Scott, 1996).[2] As will hopefully become evident in this present book, Early Modern feminism had much more than paradoxes to offer. The recent more positive approach of feminism will perhaps reduce its stereotypical reputation as only critical and negative.

A representative sample of a negative attitude towards the tradition within feminist philosophy is Susan Moller Okin's *Women in Western Political Thought* (1979), a book that primarily focuses on what canonical figures like Plato, Aristotle, Rousseau and Mill had to say about women.[3] Although a pioneering book of its sort with interesting analyses, my own approach is very different from Okin's. I do share Okin's motivation for wanting to "[comprehend] and [lay] bare the assumptions behind deeply rooted models of thought that continue to affect people's lives in major ways" (Okin, 1987: 3) but our arguments to this end take very different routes. While Okin manifests that she wants to explore Western thinking in order to pry out why the political theories of philosophers "[have] not led to substantial equality between the sexes" (ibid., 4), my ambition is to show that these theories *have* led to equality between the sexes and how these theories have made a discourse of gender equality even possible at all. Not that I would argue that full and utter gender equality is achieved anywhere – I agree that much still needs to be done – but Western societies are so far the only ones in global history that have achieved the level of equality between the sexes that we have today and in addition to that a good deal of theorization about it. And it is this phenomenon or this story that this book at hand sets out to explore. The geographical framework for this story is a European and Western context.[4]

Historical present

A question we need to ask ourselves is this: why be concerned with *history* at all rather than address contemporary problems in feminist theory? I think the answer lies in what I said above, that what has been excluded in the history of philosophy and also missing in early feminist studies is the history of feminism. This is a history, or a canon in its own right and of significant interest, that we can unveil. It is a history we ought to be familiar with and proud of. Another argument is that past resources can offer reflections of the present, they can contribute to the puzzle of understanding who we are and how we have become who we are. I also believe that seeing feminism as a product of Modernity is decisive for how we understand feminism as a project. But, most importantly, the essential argument in favour of the importance of historical consciousness and historical knowledge is that the present situation, the status quo of feminism, is marked by philosophical, political and cultural conditions and terms laid in an earlier phase.

An additional aim of this project is to show the relevance and importance of history for contemporary thinking. In Chapter 2 we shall have a closer look at the concept of equality and examine the importance of this concept for the development of modern feminism and hence also for contemporary feminist thinking. In his *Liberty Before Liberalism*, historian Quentin Skinner analyses the concept of liberty and claims that, ever since the 17th century, this concept has remained at the heart of political self-understanding and practice of the modern West. I would make the exact same claim for the concept of equality and its centrality for Western feminism. Skinner writes:

> It seems to me that most of us do not know; that we have inherited a theory which we continue to apply, but which we do not really understand. If this is so, however, then one of the ways – perhaps the only way – of improving our understanding will be to go back to the historical juncture at which this way of thinking about politics was first articulated and developed. We shall then be able to see how the concepts we still invoke were initially defined, what purposes they were intended to serve, what view of public power they were used to underpin. This in turn may enable us to acquire a self-conscious understanding of a set of concepts that we now employ unselfconsciously and, to some degree, even uncomprehendingly. It is arguable, in short, that we need to become intellectual historians if we are to make sense not merely of this but of many comparable aspects of our present moral and political world.
>
> (Skinner, 1998: 109–110)

Skinner's argument is here very Nietzschean. In *On the Genealogy of Morality*, Nietzsche sets forth to examine the origin and value of morality and for this purpose a new method is according to him required: the *genealogical* method. This method consists of tracking the historical development of concepts and/or phenomena and trying to uncover what has been forgotten or hidden during the process of development (while at the same time looking at resistance, ruptures and backlashes).

Analogous to what Skinner says about politics and liberty, I also think that feminism is a tradition with concepts we have inherited and that we will acquire greater self-consciousness if we study the history and origin of these concepts. I also follow Skinner in his argument against the idea that values of the past are values we no longer endorse, questions of the past are questions we no longer ask. "One corresponding role for the intellectual historian", Skinner writes, "is that of acting as a kind of archaeologist; bringing buried intellectual treasure back to the surface, dusting it down and enabling us to reconsider what we think of it" (ibid., page 112). In the case of feminism, the idea is not only to reconsider what we think about feminism's own history but also to illustrate the indebtedness to and relevance of past thinking for contemporary thought and that is what is sought by the reference in the subtitle to "Historical Present".

For Nietzsche it was crucial to show that morality had a history, that judgements like good and evil did not have an eternal value written in stone, but that the meaning of these judgements had changed over time and originally even perhaps had opposite meanings (Nietzsche, 2006). For Skinner it is decisive to show that liberty has a history and for the present project equally decisive to show that feminism and its central concepts like equality have a history (more on this topic in Chapter 2).

As mentioned, the purpose of this book then is to show the importance of history for contemporary feminism, and to show that feminism is a product of European Modernity. The method applied is a composite of inspiration from Nietzsche, Rorty and Skinner. History is here treated as a source and an archive where hidden material can be carved out. In this view the canon of philosophy is seen as a source and an archive more than an eternal and unchangeable *doxa*. I also read the history of philosophy as *conditions of possibility* for feminist thinking at all. The cultural critic and Egyptologist Aleida Assman calls the phenomenon canon as part of "cultural memory". Correspondingly, to individual persons the cultural memory is selective. What we forget on an individual or cultural level is not erased forever but it is placed in our sub-consciousness as an archive. "The archive is a kind of 'lost-and-found-office' for what is no longer needed or immediately understood" (Assman, 2008: 106). And from this lost-and-found-office we can reveal stories once thought lost or that no one has seen before, and here we can also find a history of feminism.

Also, Seyla Benhabib points to the necessity of carving new stories out of the history of philosophy. Benhabib joins Luce Irigaray in criticizing the canon for hiding a white, Western middle-class male:

> If the subject of the Western intellectual tradition has usually been white, Christian, male head of household, the History as hitherto recorded and narrated has been "his story". Furthermore, the various philosophies of history which have dominated since the Enlightenment have forced historical narratives unto unity, homogeneity and linearity with the consequence that fragmentation, heterogeneity and above all the varying pace of different temporalities as experienced by different groups have been obliterated. We need only remember Hegel's belief that Africa has no history. Until very recently neither did women have their own history, their own narrative with different categories of periodization and with different structural regularities.
> (Benhabib, 1992: 212)

The histories of Africa, women and feminism are all lying there waiting to be told. Giving voice to earlier hidden stories can be compared to what African-American author Toni Morrison is doing in her novels when she is giving voice to the slaves' stories or what Holberg laureate Natalie Zemon Davies does in e.g. *Women on the Margins* (1997), when history is narrated through those situated in the margins: peasants and maids.[5]

Knowledge on the history of feminist thinking is decisive for our understanding of ourselves and our present discourse on gender equality. As I see it, there are (at least) three key features connected with such a project: (a) a historicizing of feminism can bring about or occasion a renewed understanding of feminism as phenomenon and project, i.e. a product of Modernity, (b) viewing feminism as having a history of its own can liberate feminism from its status as secondary to other disciplines, and (c) ultimately, a genealogy of feminism might succeed in inscribing feminist thinking into the canon of European intellectual history.

The next five chapters will discuss thinkers and philosophical developments that all contributed to the development of modern Western feminism.

Notes

1 See e.g. Robin May Schott: 2007, 54.
2 Scott uses the term "paradoxes" to avoid presenting the history of feminism as a teleological story of progress, very much like my own approach with the term "genealogy". It is rather the adjective "only" that signals a poor outcome.
3 My point is not to criticize Okin but to illustrate different approaches to the same material. This difference of approach is probably linked to generational differences.
4 I am well aware of post-colonial theory and criticism, but I will argue that it is not relevant for this project.
5 Zemon Davis was awarded the prize in 2010. The Holberg Prize is an international prize awarded annually by the government of Norway to outstanding scholars for work in the arts, humanities and social sciences, law and theology. The prize is named after Danish-Norwegian writer and academic Ludvig Holberg (1684–1754). For a short entry on Ludvig Holberg, see Chapter 3.

1 Feminism as a modern phenomenon

Modernity revisited

This chapter will primarily discuss what the term "feminism" refers to. What is feminism? Secondly, it will defend an understanding of feminism as a legitimate child and product of Modernity. And, thirdly, the chapter ends with an exploration of the historization of feminism.

The history of feminism is often portrayed with a metaphor of three waves, the first wave being the one initiated by the British suffragettes. This metaphor of waves will hereby be challenged, as it is inadequate to describe the overall phenomenon, and in particular because it obscures the epoch prior to the French Revolution. The metaphor of three waves does not capture feminism as a product of Modernity. The development and progress of Modernity made it possible to dismiss tradition in favour of new and "better" ideas, and it is this understanding of Modernity that will be followed here. The chapter will also explore what differentiates *modern* feminism from pre-modern (and anti-modern). Modernity has been defined as "an historical period following the middle ages. It is a post-traditional order marked by change, innovation and dynamism" (Barker, 2000: 187).

Several thinkers have tried to deal with the problematic consequences of Modernity. In one sense all philosophy since Descartes has been a discourse on the problems of Modernity, be it Kantian "autonomy", Hegelian "Absolute Spirit" or Nietzschean "death of God". Modernity, or post-medieval Europe on this understanding, represents the idea or sense that the present is discontinuous with the past. Modernity therefore represents a break with the past and tradition, a development that began in the Renaissance. It is defined by the emergence of mechanical science, global exploration, inventions, the Reformation, the Enlightenment, the arrival of the printing press, the French Revolution, the rise of the nation-state, industrialization, the rise of capitalism, social movements and equality politics, mass literacy, to mention but a few factors.

12 *Feminism as a modern phenomenon*

As a historical period, Modernity is identified as post-traditional and post-medieval, which again is identified by a move from feudalism toward capitalism, industrialization, secularization and rationalization. The period disintegrates from previous religious world views, which are replaced by revolutionary discoveries within science, theories of morality and law grounded on principles, and autonomous art, to mention a few. According to Jürgen Habermas, the discovery of the "new world", the Renaissance, and the Reformation were the three monumental events around the year 1500 that constituted the epochal threshold between modern times and the Middle Ages (Habermas, 1987). Modernity implies a decisive break in an intellectual tradition and an inability to rely on assumptions and practices taken for granted in the past. Modernity no longer takes its bearings from earlier models but seeks to regulate and evaluate beliefs through rational self-reflection. "The *autonomous* rule" of our own thoughts liberates us from interest, tradition and prejudice. Feminism in itself is part of this break with tradition and a true product of Modernity. When tradition and prejudice lose sway, relations between the sexes can be approached anew. Modernity is a "multifaceted theme", as Habermas terms it; all the same, he writes 400 pages on the philosophical discourse of Modernity without even mentioning the radical changes of women's condition and in the relationship between the sexes. The ambition of this book is to solidly secure feminism a place in the discourse of Modernity.

Aristotelian scholastics had argued that women's *nature* made them inferior to men; this view is challenged by Modernity. Explanation is no longer sought in nature, but in observations and experience. And observation and experience show that women are capable of more than cooking and sewing. René Descartes is often referred to as the father of modern philosophy; what is *modern* in his thinking is his break with tradition and insistence on rational arguments based on cognitive experience. Dissatisfied with the education he had been given, Descartes presented the theory wherein the *method* is the foundation of scientific truth rather than the tradition and handed over truths. Truth is based on method and rational arguments truth arrives from a chain of indubitable premises. For Aristotle, women were secondary to men, or subordinate to men, because of their nature. He thought nature had created women less important and with less mental and moral capacity than men. According to him, a woman was an imperfect or incomplete man. Early Modern thinkers like Marie de Gournay and Poulain de la Barre claim on the contrary that sexual difference is culturally produced. The differences between men and women are due to differences in education and upbringing. Gender is no longer understood exclusively by tradition and nature; Modernity brings observation, arguments and culture to the table.

Feminism as a modern phenomenon 13

All delimitations of beginnings and endings of historical periods are to some extent arbitrary. It can nevertheless be of use in identifying certain events as initiating or terminating an epoch, which often helps one to understand and organize the events within that span of time. This book is an attempt to map the beginning of modern feminism, or *a* beginning of modern feminism, rather than *the* beginning of modern feminism. Perhaps even better expressed in plural; the beginning*s* of modern feminism. At the same time the book's ambition is to show the relevance of this beginning for contemporary feminist thought.

The epoch of modern philosophy is said to begin with the publication of Descartes' *Meditations on First Philosophy* in 1641. The year 1641 also saw the publication of another text; Marie le Jars de Gournay's *On the Equality of Men and Women*, which signalled the beginning of another product of Modernity; modern feminism.[1] In the chapters to come I will argue that modern feminism is (a) centred around concepts of equality and difference, (b) characterized by rational arguments rather than theological explanation and interpretation and thus (c) it is also secular and perhaps most importantly (d) an autonomous i.e. a critical system of thought in its own right. Being modern also means that it is a tradition we can recognize and still be in dialogue with, or, put the other way around, it is a tradition that is still in dialogue with us; it still speaks to us. The point is not to claim that there weren't any pre-modern feminist initiatives, there certainly were several, but these did not lead to any significant change for women on a broader scale, and some of them, like Christine de Pizan, are written within a world picture or cosmology that is very different and even alien to ours. But still one might wonder why it matters whether or when modern feminism began. I would answer that giving feminism its proper history is to give it a place in the world. As the historian Miri Rubin writes: "The quest for origins is a quest for a place in the world, it is an exercise in self-definition, self-understanding and self-fashioning" (Rubin, 1889: 34). By the 21st century feminism has become mainstream, most Western societies have incorporated gender equality as a goal and ideal, and feminism has even turned academic with numerous centres for gender-studies and academic degrees in feminist subjects. Feminism has reached a point where it can make a turn and reflect upon itself both for the sake of self-understanding and self-reflection and for the sake of demanding recognition and a place in the world. It is time to acknowledge that feminism or gender equality is an equally essential characteristic of Western thought and culture as the belief in scientific truth, democracy, freedom of speech and human rights to mention but a few modern achievements.

14 *Feminism as a modern phenomenon*

The F-word – what is feminism?

"I myself have never been able to find out precisely what feminism is: I only know that people call me a feminist whenever I express sentiments that differentiate me from a doormat", wrote British author, journalist and feminist Rebecca West in 1913.[2] In the perspective of the history of modern feminism, the term "feminism" is of a rather late date and is believed to be of French origin. The first registered use, according to historian of feminism Karen Offen, is from around the 1870s. The exact origin of the term is uncertain. Some scholars tie it to Hubertine Auclert, the founder of the first suffrage society in France (Cott, 1987: 14), others to the French Utopian socialist Charles Fourier (Rendall, 1985: 1). The term travelled from France to England and did not enter everyday language until it was used to describe the British suffragettes in 1908–1909. The conceptual innovation of introducing the term "feminism" was part of a larger re-formulation of political movements as "isms", e.g. nationalism, liberalism and socialism. In other words, "feminism" is a 19th century conceptual innovation.

If we distinguish feminism as (a) a social and political movement from (b) a set of ideas we can argue that it makes good sense to use the term "feminism" to describe all efforts to overthrow gender hierarchy, also those that took place prior to the invention of the term, like the Renaissance or Early Modernity. And it is feminism understood as ideas, and not feminism as a socio-political movement that is the topic if this book.

The term is made up by the Latin word for woman, *femin-a*, added to the suffix *ism*. The ism-suffix usually points to an ideology that presupposes a set of principles. The tying together of the two terms caused confusion in the United States: was this an ideology that men could join or a separate and antagonistic politics for women only, perhaps even threatening men with feminization (Cott, 1987: 15)?

Oxford English Dictionary defines feminism as: "Advocacy of the rights of women (based on the theory of equality of the sexes)" and lists "womanism" as an alternative term. Karen Offen writes that feminism "connote[s] the ideas that advocate the emancipation of women, the movements have attempted to realize it" (Offen, 2000: 19). Sally Haslanger and Nancy Tuana define feminism as "an umbrella term for a range of views about injustices against women" and claim that feminists are committed to bringing about social change to end injustice against women, in particular, injustice against women as women (Haslanger & Tuana, 2012). In 2008 Alison Jaggar defined feminism as: "a cluster of social and political ideals that continuously evolve and change" and "an activity directed toward promoting justice and equality" (Jaggar, 2008: vii).

Publicly debating the position of women is, however, neither a new nor modern phenomenon. The so-called *querelle des femmes* (the quarrel about women) brought several writers and thinkers, male and female, to enter the debate, among others the Dano-Norwegian writer and proto-feminist Ludvig Holberg (1684–1754), who wrote a history of famous women and coined the term "gynaicologia" for the enterprise of defending women.

The term feminism can also be misused, as Judith Butler points out in her book *Frames of War* (Butler, 2009). Here Butler criticizes the Bush administration for presenting the war in Afghanistan as a women's liberation war. Consequently, Afghanistan was bombed in order to liberate women from the burka and the Taliban, and feminism was re-written into geopolitical war rhetoric. This is outright misuse and co-optation of feminism, according to Butler.

People often ask for a definition of what feminism actually or really is, and although the plural term *feminisms* might be most accurate, I think the following definition covers at least a common multiple: Feminism is a view that (1) women and the feminine are systematically subordinated to men and the masculine, and (2) that gender and gender-roles and the relation between the sexes are not predetermined by any natural and unchangeable essences, but (3) are something that can be changed by social-cultural revisions and arrangements.

The belief and wish for change is what makes feminism an equally political and philosophical project. Philosopher and feminist Nancy Fraser claims that gender must be viewed bi-focally, through two lenses at the same time (Fraser, 2007: 23–35). According to Fraser, gender is a two-dimensional category rooted simultaneously in the economic structure and in the status order of society. For Fraser, these two perspectives are equally important for what she calls "gender justice". The two are relatively independent categories, and *one* cannot constitute a remedy for the *other*. Thus, feminism needs both empirical inquiries as well as philosophical analyses. A major feature of gender injustice is androcentrism, Fraser argues, which entails an institutionalized pattern of cultural value that privileges traits associated with masculinity, while devaluing everything coded as "feminine". For Fraser the essential questions of feminism can be summed up in two central concepts: *redistribution* (of political power and economy) and *recognition* (in the cultural-discursive perspective).

Seyla Benhabib offers, in my view, an illuminating definition of feminist theory in her *Situating the Self*. She claims that feminist theory operates on two levels, empirical and philosophical. The task of feminist theory, she suggests, is to uncover how the historically known gender-sex systems have contributed to the oppression and exploitation of women and simultaneously develop a theory that is emancipatory and reflective. This can be done in two ways, either by an "explanatory-diagnostic analysis", which is social, scientific or empirical, or by articulating "anticipatory utopian critique of the norms and values of our current society", which is primarily "normative and philosophical" (Benhabib, 1992).

A few words on philosophy and feminism: just like philosophy, feminism entails a variety of perspectives, conceptual frameworks and methods. The intertwinement of *feminism* and *philosophy* appears perhaps to some as either an oxymoron or a *contradictio in adjecto*, where the alliance is seen as an unhappy, forced marriage between the particular and the universal, the concrete and the abstract, the political and the scientific, or between change and constancy. The perhaps most unfortunate attitude against connecting philosophy and feminism is the widespread misconception that feminist theory is theory *by, about* and *for* women. This view derives perhaps from feminist standpoint theory, which posits feminism as a way of conceptualizing from the vantage point of women's life and experience, e.g. Nancy Hartsock and Sandra Harding's thinking. Standpoint theory derives from the Marxist position that the socially oppressed classes can access knowledge unavailable to the socially privileged, particularly knowledge of social relations. Standpoint theory becomes controversial when it claims epistemic privilege over the perspectives of the groups that dominate them. Feminist standpoint theory has received substantial criticism from within, e.g. from Helen Longino. The point I want to make, however, is that men have been, still are and will continue to be feminists. A history of feminist thinking includes several male contributors such as Michel de Montaigne, René Descartes, François Poulain de la Barre, John Locke, Ludvig Holberg, Marquis de Condorcet and John Stuart Mill.

Anti-feminism(s)

One of the reasons for the lack of knowledge of feminism's history is due to a general and strong anti-feminism attitude. In order to understand how feminism has progressed and developed it might be equally useful trying to understand how it has been opposed and attacked. Virginia Woolf writes in *A Room of One's Own*: "The history of men's opposition to women's emancipation is more interesting perhaps than the story of that emancipation itself" (Woolf, 2008: 72). Describing the reception of *The Second*

Sex in her autobiography *Force of Circumstance*, Simone de Beauvoir writes that she was accused of being "Unsatisfied, frigid, priapic, nymphomaniac, lesbian, a hundred times aborted, I was everything, even an unmarried mother" (Beauvoir, 1994: 97). Several feminists have experienced being unfairly attacked for their views. Mary Wollstonecraft was e.g. referred to as "hyena in petticoats", "the foremost among modern-day *unsexed females*" and the *Anti-Jacobin Review* of 1798 went so far as to index her under "P" for prostitute.[3] Marie de Gournay was a victim of practical jokes, gossip and slander, which made her publish a detailed defence justifying her role and situation as a learned woman. In *Apology for the Woman Writing*, she writes:

> [T]hey fantastically prank up the image of an educated woman – that is, they make of her a stew of extravagancies and chimeras, and they say in general, without bothering with exceptions and distinctions, that such women are shaped on this mold. Whatever may present itself beyond this stereotype to disprove her conformity to it, those vulgar people in no way understand her, and she is no longer seen except in the light of wrongful presumptions and as the image of such a scarecrow.
>
> (Gournay, 2002: 124)

Beauvoir, Wollstonecraft and Gournay alike lived their lives in ways untraditional for women of their day, something that did not go unheeded. The attacks on these women are equally directed at their lifestyles as at their feminist opinions. To understand the hostility towards feminism, one might pick up on what feminist sociologist Sara Ahmed calls "feminist killjoy". In challenging ideas about gender, feminists also challenge how happiness is defined, according to Ahmed (Ahmed, 2010: 581). Ahmed also identifies a desire to believe that women become feminists because they are unhappy. Being joyless and sad, feminists kill joy. Reading feminists as unhappy takes the focus away from what feminists are unhappy about, Ahmed writes. Simone de Beauvoir expresses a similar attitude when she says that she was never treated as a target for sarcasm until after the publication of *The Second Sex* – before that people were either indifferent or kind to her:

> Afterwards I was often attacked as a woman because my attackers thought it must be my Achilles' heel; but I knew perfectly well that this persistent petulance was really aimed at my moral and social convictions. No; far from suffering from my femininity, I have, on

the contrary, from the age of twenty on, accumulated the advantages of both sexes […].

(Beauvoir, 1994: 199)

Beauvoir here hits the nail on the head; anti-feminists think that feminists' sore point is their femininity – because they are ugly and unable to attract men, they become feminists. A particularly vicious attack of this sort is the example earlier mentioned, where Wollstonecraft was indexed under P for prostitute. Many feminists have probably, at some point or another, met with the attitude that they are feminists because of some deficiency in their femininity.

Beauvoir also reports other reactions to *The Second Sex* where men wanted to know what she had against them. "Nothing; I had nothing against anything except the words I was quoting. It is strange that so many intellectuals should refuse to believe in intellectual passions" (ibid., 200). Feminism is not targeted against men as individuals but against a system that subordinates women. This system is equally upheld by men as well as by women, thus Beauvoir and Wollstonecraft place the responsibility to overthrow the gender hierarchy on both sexes. Part of the problem, as they see it, is that women are partly responsible for their own subordination. Still many men feel personally attacked by feminism, to cite Beauvoir again:

> Most men took as a personal insult the information I retailed about frigidity in women; they wanted to imagine that they could dispense pleasure whenever and whomever they pleased; to doubt such powers on their part was to castrate them.
>
> (ibid.)

Beauvoir was a killjoy killing their happy fantasies, in the words of Sara Ahmed.

Early Modern feminists were also likewise attacked and ridiculed. Marie le Jars de Gournay was the victim of ridicule and practical jokes and was derogatorily referred to as an "old maid", and as in the case of Beauvoir and Wollstonecraft it is her femininity rather than her writing and arguments that are attacked. Karen Offen writes that "the critique levelled at the 'learned ladies' of Elizabethan England, and especially at the *femmes savants* of mid-seventeenth-century Parisian high society, was vicious and unprecedented" (Offen, 2000: 37), as is reflected in Molière's widely known comedies *Les Précieuses ridicules* (1659) and *Les Femmes savants* (1672). These strong forces against feminism have not just delayed and obstructed the development of overthrowing gender hierarchy but have led to a forgetting and cover-up of feminist history.

Forgetting and remembering

"Let us not forget", Luce Irigaray argues "that we already have a history, that certain women, despite all the cultural obstacles, have made their mark upon history and all too often have been forgotten by us" (Irigaray, 1993: 19). French-Belgian feminist philosopher Luce Irigaray is celebrated for her creative re-readings of canonical texts and thinkers. Her philosophical project is to uncover the absence of a female subject position in Western culture and history of philosophy. Like Seyla Benhabib, mentioned earlier, Irigaray accuses the history of philosophy of being a male subject in disguise. But even Luce Irigaray, who points out that women have made their mark upon history, is guilty of contributing to the neglect of women, albeit perhaps unwillingly. Her lack of attention to female philosophers contributes to reinforcing the canon as a line of kings and great men. For someone who emphasizes the importance of female genealogies, it is striking that she never applies her creative re-readings to any women nor ever refers to any intellectual foremothers. Irigaray's innovative re-readings of the history of philosophy includes thinkers like Plato, Aristotle, Descartes, Spinoza, Hegel, Nietzsche, Heidegger, Levinas and Merleau-Ponty. When she exclusively focuses on a male canon of philosophy, the following question is unavoidable: is Irigaray thus contributing to strengthening the picture of this tradition as an exclusively male enterprise?

Another feminist thinker, Julia Kristeva, was criticized in a similar way for basing her analyses exclusively on male thinkers and authors. Kristeva answered this critique by focusing precisely on female genius and wrote three intellectual biographies of Hannah Arendt, Melanie Klein and Colette.

Indeed, Irigaray refers to both Diotima and Antigone, two prominent female figures in the history of philosophy, but that is also all that they are, *figures* or metaphors, and not really philosophers, even though some claim Diotima in actual fact is a historical person, known as Diotima of Mantinea.[4] Irigaray only refers to the fictive character created by Plato. In Irigaray, Antigone and Diotima only fill the function Michele le Doeuff has called "philosophical imaginary", i.e. images that point to something other than themselves (le Doeuff, 1989).[5] In Irigaray's texts, one looks in vain for Mary Wollstonecraft, Olympe de Gouges, Marie de Gournay, Mary Astell or Christine de Pizan, to mention some of the female thinkers that could have figured in a female genealogy. And even if she sometimes mentions Simone de Beauvoir, it is primarily to distance herself from Beauvoir. Irigaray's repeated critique of philosophy's great male names is that they do not acknowledge their debt to the female. It is thus almost ironic that Irigaray herself never explicitly acknowledges any debt to any woman.

Every time a male canonical thinker is read as such, his position as canonical is reinforced, even if the reading is critical. There is an invisible "nothing succeeds like success" logic that in addition to philosophical criteria contributes to defining the canon of philosophy. My critical objection to Irigaray is that she, albeit unwillingly, contributes to the understanding of philosophy as a male privilege, and is guilty of making female voices, from the past as well as from the present, invisible.

Paraphrasing art historian Linda Nochlin's famous question from 1971, "Why have there been no great women artists?" (Nochlin, 1971), we could ask why there have been no great women thinkers or scientists. But the question is rather: why have we heard so little about them or why have they been forgotten, which is exactly Nochlin's take on women artists. The point is not to claim that there have been just as many female thinkers as male thinkers, but that there have been *some* and that many of these have been forgotten. Feminism is not a cumulative enterprise, it is just as much a story of lost ideas as creation of new ones. A historical perspective on feminism must thus try to remember these lost women and their ideas.

Beauvoir's canon of feminism

A 20th century feminist who was quite conscious concerning the history of feminism is Simone de Beauvoir. In the "History" chapter of *The Second Sex* she maps out a "canon of feminism", beginning with the Renaissance and Christine de Pisan, which demonstrates an understanding of feminism as a historical project. In Beauvoir scholarship this chapter is oddly enough one of the least commented upon. But it is not only in Beauvoir scholarship that her canon of feminism is overlooked. Few, if any, historians of feminism refer to this aspect of Beauvoir's work. This could be explained by the fact that they are historians and not philosophers and thus do not read Beauvoir, but it is still quite peculiar that they "forget" Beauvoir in this connection, given that it is precisely the history of feminism they are engaged with. Joan Kelly is often credited for having been the first to point to a feminist tradition that preceded the French Revolution, but Beauvoir anticipates Kelly by more than 30 years.

Philosophical readings of *The Second Sex* on the other hand tend to be more thematic than systematic, which might explain why Beauvoir's historiography of feminism has received less attention among philosophers and Beauvoir scholars. The standard themes associated with Beauvoir seem to be the sexed body, freedom, woman as the other, phenomenology and master/slave-dialectic. The commentary literature's interest in ethic and ontological perspectives overshadows Beauvoir's historical philosophy.

The Second Sex occupies a central place in the history of feminism, but the book itself also presents *its* own version of the history of feminism, with a primary focus on French 16th and 17th century thinking. This is not an expression of nationalism on behalf of Beauvoir. Paris was the intellectual capital of Europe in the 16th and 17th centuries. It is thus not only in Beauvoir's account of the history of feminism that France occupies a central role in the Early Modern period, but also in all other accounts. French was the English of that time and books published in French circulated all over Europe. According to Beauvoir, Christine de Pizan's writings represent the first time a woman took up her pen to defend her sex (Beauvoir, 2011: 120). Christine de Pizan countered the misogyny of Jean de Meun's *Le Roman de Rose*. The literary debate that grew out of this novel is the origin of the *querelle des femmes*, or the quarrel on women. Written in the 13th century, the *Roman de Rose* promotes the view that women are nothing but cynical seductresses of men. Nothing but slander, wrote Pizan.

Beauvoir also mentions Mary Wollstonecraft and her *Vindication of the Rights of Woman* and claims that it was Wollstonecraft who sparked the women's movement in England. There are notably several similarities between Beauvoir's introduction to *The Second Sex* and Wollstonecraft's introduction to *Vindication*. They both take as their point of departure the same statement – "I am a woman" – i.e. they both aim for a synthesis between the personal and the philosophical. For the Beauvoir scholar Toril Moi this is a unique feature of Beauvoir, but I will suggest that Beauvoir is more influenced by Wollstonecraft than Beauvoir perhaps liked to admit.

Beauvoir's historical project is not purely historical but an attempt at combining or connecting Existential philosophy with historical analyses. Hence Beauvoir analyzes women's situation in history through concrete phenomena such as pregnancy, childbirth, contraception, abortion, divorce, education, class, the origin of feminism and the backlash of feminism.[6] Dutch philosopher Karen Vintges claims that it is not Beauvoir's intention to present a reductive biological understanding of woman. According to Vintges, Beauvoir's central theses in *The Second Sex* is woman as *historic* Other (1998: 209). Exploring the historic situation of women, Beauvoir concluded that they had been prevented from controlling their own lives and exercising their freedom. Woman had been the Other throughout history and man the Self, the Subject. Thus history, and the history of feminism, play a crucial role in Beauvoir's project.

By listing many of her predecessors, male as well as female, Beauvoir recognized their influence, which again demonstrates that she was not exclusively influenced by male philosophers. Beauvoir's text is full of voices of women who are her predecessors and contemporaries, from Mary Wollstonecraft to Susan B. Anthony, from Mme de Staël to Virginia Woolf.

Among these voices we find Marie de Gournay. Beauvoir does indeed have a reference to her, but not in the first English version of *The Second Sex*, translated by H. M. Parshley. Parshley was a professor of zoology and in his English translation he changed some of the philosophical concepts and vocabulary and left out names mentioned in the original text. Among many changes he made to the text was deleting the reference to Gournay.

Parshley's omissions are crucial; the deletion of reference to Gournay as well as the deletion of the credit given to Poulain de la Barre on the title page cause problems for any serious historical study of feminism. Such omissions contribute to isolating *The Second Sex* from its feminist theoretical foundations. A new English translation of Beauvoir's *The Second Sex* was carried out by Constance Borde and Sheila Malovany-Chevallier in 2011. This new translation is complete and leaves nothing out, and it also sets out to restore Beauvoir's Existentialist vocabulary, which was partly omitted in the first translation.

This "exceptionalism", a tendency within much feminist scholarship to present certain women as exceptional, can cause isolation of the feminist thinker at hand. Presenting a feminist thinker as a pioneer might do her a disservice if this pioneering thinking is presented as separate from contemporary thinking. Not reading feminist thinkers as part of their own present, history and philosophical context risks reducing them to curiosities whose ideas have expired. This, it seems to me, is particularly the case in readings of Wollstonecraft and Beauvoir; holding them up as exceptional pioneers risks removing them from the mainstream history of intellectual ideas. In other words, treating them as exceptional and pioneers only marginalizes them further.

Notes

1 Gournay's pamphlet was first printed in 1622, but it is the revised version of 1641 that is the standard translated version.
2 *The Clarion*, November 14, 1913.

3 See Claudia L. Johnson's "Introduction" in *The Cambridge Companion to Mary Wollstonecraft*, edited by Claudia L. Johnson, Cambridge University Press, 2002. Thanks to colleague Tone Brekke for bringing my attention to this.
4 See Mary Ellen Waithe (ed.): *A History of Women Philosophers* vol. 1–4, Martinus Nijhoff Publishers, Dordrecht, Boston, Lancaster, 1987–1995.
5 According to le Doeuff there is an extensive use of images in philosophical rhetoric. These images are used to strengthen arguments and thoughts, but also to hide contradictions and weak thinking.
6 E.g. Code Napoléon, which gave men complete control over wife and children.

2 Philosophies of equality

The problem of equality

The concept of equality is one of the most central concepts within feminism as well as in political theory. Equality is a fundamental concept for any theory of justice and democracy alike. However, there are few academic studies or examinations of the origin and historical development of the concept. It is one of those concepts we take for granted as if it has always been there, as if it has perpetual and self-evident meaning. Little attention is paid to the fact that equality as a social and political idea is a fairly recent concept and is one of the products of Early Modern European Enlightenment thinking. Even less attention is given to the fact that feminism or the idea of gender equality runs parallel with and even anticipates the general development of a philosophical and political concept of equality. This lack of systematic study has also been pointed out by other scholars, e.g. historian Siep Stuurman and historian of ideas Jonathan I. Israel. Stuurman suggests that history of political thought ought to include a "history of equality" (Stuurman, 2000: 147–166) and Israel writes:

> Among the most divisive and potentially perplexing of all basic concepts introduced by the Radical Enlightenment into the make-up of modernity, and one of the most revolutionary in its implications, was, and is, the idea of equality. Assertion of universal and fundamental equality was undoubtedly central not just to the Radical Enlightenment but to the entire structure of democratic values espoused by the modern West. Yet, neither the philosophical nor the historical grounding of this idea, that is its intellectual origins and roots, is at all obvious and this whole issue has been, to a quite remarkable extent, shrouded in neglect in historical academic literature.
>
> (Israel, 2006: 545)

Also, Jeremy Waldron comments in his book *God, Locke and Equality* that "although there is plenty of work on equality, there is precious little in modern literature on the background idea that we humans are, fundamentally, one another's equals" (Waldron, 2002: 2). This is also true in the case of feminist literature, where work focusing on the concept of equality is scarce. This chapter will take up the challenge and try to uncover and release some of the important aspects of the philosophical history behind the modern idea of equality.

The chapter will first go through some general points about equality and its origin from mathematics before special attention is given to Marie le Jars de Gournay (1565–1645), who in this book will be proclaimed as the founder of modern feminism. From Gournay we move to Montaigne and the modern idea of subjectivity and finally to a discussion of equality and education. Most feminists have felt, and many still argue, that lack of education is the source of women's inequality and hence that improvement of education for women is the solution to the problem.

Although the notion of equality has been used in social and moral contexts for centuries, this is not the notion's original "home" (Hajdin, 2001). The primary use of the notion of equality stems from mathematics, where equality is considered as a relationship between numbers signifying identity between quantities. When used to describe a relationship between humans, equality no longer refers to quantity but quality. Equality represents a *qualitative* relationship between humans. As a mathematical notion equality is quite easy to define, while when it enters moral and political debates it becomes quite difficult to give a precise definition of what is meant by the term, a problem also identified by the Indian economist Amartya Sen when asking: "Equality of what?" (Sen, 1980). Trying to define equality, we soon end up with the problem identified by British philosopher Bernard Williams in his 1962 essay "The idea of equality" (Williams, 1973). According to Williams, the concept of equality is used in two ways. In political discussions the idea of equality is used both as (a) statements of facts, that men *are* equal, and in (b) statements of political aims that men *should be* equal, as at present they are not. There are thus two types of equality, descriptive and prescriptive, basic equality and equality as an aim.

So, what do we actually *mean* by "equality"? Do we mean equal status, equal rights or equal possibilities? Is it a question of law, politics or ethics? Is it a question of quantity or quality, equal representation or equal status? Or is it perhaps a question of resources and economic equality? And how do we measure equality – is 50/50 the ultimate ideal? Should differences be treated equally or differently? These are just a few of the many undefended questions following in the wake of equality. Equality proves to be a complicated philosophical notion; its sweeping complexity will, however, not be pursued in depth here other than as treated by central feminists, but we can keep in the back of our heads that we are dealing with a complex notion. In the words of Alison Jaggar, the concept of equality is "notoriously elusive" (Jaggar, 1974).

There are two ways of approaching equality philosophically; one is by historical analysis, the other by systematic or analytical account. This chapter will focus primarily on the philosophical history of equality with some additional theoretical reflection. As for the wider importance of the equality concept, Amartya Sen claims that equality was not only among the foremost revolutionary demands in 18th century Europe and America, but there has also been an extraordinary consensus on its importance in post-Enlightenment world (Sen, 2010). The United Nations Sustainability Goals confirm the over-all consensus of its importance.[1] Equality is a worldwide and global ideal with a European Enlightenment origin. In general, it is thinkers like John Locke and Thomas Hobbes who are credited for the relevant idea of equality. But in the case of equality, feminism is, in fact, ahead of mainstream philosophy. In 1624, Marie le Jars de Gournay first published her pamphlet *The Equality of Men and Women*, which is probably the very first proposal for gender equality in modern Europe. This shows that one must not only ask what the significance of Enlightenment philosophy for feminism was, but also what the significance of feminism for Enlightenment philosophy and egalitarianism was (Akkerman & Stuurman, 1998).

Ever since Marie le Jars de Gournay first proposed equality between the sexes in 1624/1641, the idea of equality has developed as one of the fundamental concepts within Western feminism. We can thus speak of a shift of paradigm initiated by Gournay, in the sense introduced by Thomas Kuhn in his influential *The Structure of Scientific Revolution* from 1962, i.e. a change in basic assumptions within ruling theory. Ruling theory in Gournay's time was that men and women were basically unequal. Men and women were not only unequal but following the pro-woman and anti-woman sides in the *querelle des femmes*, women were either better or worse than men.

The *querelle des femmes* or dispute about women was a European debate concerning the moral status and role of women that lasted for at least two centuries. Some claim that the *querelle* ended with Gournay (O'Neill, 2007), others that it lasted until the French Revolution (Kelly, 1982).[2] However, it is customary to claim that it began with Christine de Pizan (1365–1431) and the literary debate following Jean de Meun's misogynistic *Roman de la Rose*. The Renaissance and Early

Modernity's notion of woman is marked by a low assessment of the female sex, writings focus on the vices and failings of women.

> Moralistic writing at this time is marked by a deep distrust of woman's nature, a belief in her tendency to err, coupled with a critical attitude to her behaviour in society and to her preference of the pleasures of this world to the task of preparing for the next.
>
> (Maclean, 1977)

A widespread view was that women were born inferior to men and therefore destined to live under male guidance and control (Fairchilds, 2007). Much ink floated in the wake of the *querelle*. Arguments came from all sides, from the idea that women were not even human,[3] to the idea that women were actually superior to men. Accusations were launched *against* women while others *defended* women, discussions focused on whether women should be educated, be allowed to participate in politics, possess property, as well as what restrictions they should be under, whether women could be virtuous or whether they were born sinful and without self-control.[4] Some claimed that women had an insatiable sexual appetite and thus needed to be controlled. Natural female inferiority needed superior male control. All through the period it was frequently discussed whether the soul, the mind or reason was sexed or not, and whether women had capacity for education as well as for morals. The debate was characterized by arguments either in favour of women's excellence as in the example of German Cornelius Agrippa – magician, theologian, astrologist and alchemist who in 1529 published *De nobilitate et praecellentia foeminei sexus*, in which he argues in favour of women's theological and moral superiority. Or vice versa as in the example of Alexis Trousset, who in his *Alphabet de l'imperfection et malice des femmes* from 1617 draws examples from the Bible as "proof" of women's folly and vice. This book was a veritable success and was reprinted in 18 new editions before 1650. Women were accordingly seen as either better or worse than men. Gournay is the first to suggest that they might be *equal*.

The *querelle des femmes* runs in many ways parallel to the *querelle des anciens et moderns*, in which the contentious issue is whether to be guided by and follow values and views with origin in the tradition, i.e. goes back to Antiquity, or whether tradition must give way to new and "better" ideas. In mainstream philosophy, this break with tradition is indicated by Descartes' thinking; within feminism it is indicated by Gournay's.

28 Philosophies of equality

The role of mathematical equality

"Equality" as a concept gradually entered politics and philosophy and with this its meaning slightly, but no less importantly, changed. It took on the meaning of the condition of having equal dignity, rank, or privileges with one's peers; or simply the fact of being on an equal footing. While mathematical equality is *quantitative*, social equality is *qualitative*. It is this understanding of equality that lies behind the American Declaration of Independence: "all men are created equal" and the motto of the French Revolution: *"Liberté, égalité et fraternité"* – "Liberty, equality and brotherhood".

Its origin from mathematics might be explained by a desire on the part of Early Modern philosophers to be scientific. Historian of ideas Isaiah Berlin writes, for example, that notions like power, justice, equality, and the like were regarded as being principles answerable in the same way as more obvious factual questions such as "What is water composed of?", "How many stars are there?", "When did Julius Caesar die?" etc. (Berlin, 1998: 170). Politics, philosophy and social science were believed to be answerable with the same level of accuracy and clarity as developed within the new sciences. For Hobbes, geometry was the science par excellence, and for Descartes who was himself a practicing mathematician it was mathematics.[5] In 1557 the Welsh mathematician Robert Record invented the equals sign (=). Record is also credited for introducing algebra to England. His book *The Whetstone of Witte*, in which he introduces the equals sign, was also the first book in England to use the plus and minus symbols. Before the modern equals sign, equality was expressed with a word (Cajori, 1993: 297).[6] Robert Record was not the only one trying to coin a symbol for equality. Several mathematicians of the period had other suggestions; even Descartes tried to coin a symbol of equality. In Descartes' mathematical notations the symbol for equality resembles the letter æ and had many proponents before Record's symbol became default or standard. To what extent this "invention" or focus and effort to find a symbol of mathematical equation influenced the development of political and philosophical understanding of equality is difficult to determine.[7]

However, we must admit that there are several factors behind a shift in collective consciousness, if algebra and equation was the latest in mathematics it is reasonable to imagine that these ideas travelled to other academic areas as well. The route from one discipline to another was shorter then than now, e.g. Robert Record was a physician *and* a mathematician, Descartes was a mathematician *and* a philosopher,

John Locke was a physician *and* political thinker. The present "Berlin wall" between the humanities and the natural sciences did not exist in the 17th century. Thus, the shift in collective consciousness that gave rise to feminism and the liberation of women originates perhaps from mathematics. The gradual introduction of equality as an essential concept is confirmed by etymology. Consulting *Oxford English Dictionary* and *Dictionnaire étymologique du français* we find that the first registered uses of "equality" and "égalité" were in the 14th century. From the 15th century onwards the use of the concept increases, also in political and philosophical contexts. According to *OED* the anglicizing of the Latin *æquâlis* takes place in the 14th and 15th centuries when *equality* became an English word.

We must also take into consideration that areas where the concept was not explicitly used also helped in developing the concept, e.g. Descartes' egalitarian epistemology. His *Discourse on the Method* (1641) begins with the words: "Good sense is the most evenly distributed thing in the world", meaning: rationality is equally granted upon us all, we all have the same rational capacities. The feminist legacy of Descartes' thinking will be further explored in the next chapter. Also, John Locke's empiricism can be interpreted as egalitarian epistemology in the sense of gender-neutral epistemology, as we shall see later in Chapter 4. This in contrast to e.g. Aristotle who thought that women had less cognitive capacity.

The idea or principle of equality was in the 17th century so radical that it was conceived as something potentially dangerous. Jeremy Waldon compares the reception of equality to the reception of communism in 1950s America (Waldron, 2002). The idea of equality was regarded as unsound and dangerous to the point of incendiary, and the last thing respectable people would support. Criticisms of e.g. Gournay's support for monarchy, or Locke's lack of explicit defence of women, must be seen in this context. These thinkers were extraordinary radical in their time and we are indebted to their courage. Historian of ideas Jonathan Israel describes the Enlightenment process as "a revolution of the mind" (Israel, 2010). Ideas like democracy, racial and sexual equality; individual liberty of lifestyle; full freedom of thought, expression, and the press; eradication of religious authority from legislative process and education; and full separation of church and state are according to Israel the principles behind what he calls Radical Enlightenment (ibid.). In the context of liberal democracies, these principles no longer seem radical today, but when they were first developed they were revolutionary, i.e. they represented a dramatically new way of viewing the world.

Marie le Jars de Gournay and equality

> Most of those who take up the cause of women, opposing the arrogant preference for themselves that is asserted by men, give them full value for money, for they redirect the preference to them. For my part, I fly all extremes; I am content to make them equal to men, given that nature, too, is as greatly opposed, in this respect, to superiority as to inferiority.
>
> (Gournay, [1641] 2002: 75)

These are the opening words of the probably very first proposal for gender equality in modern Europe.[8] Less than 200 years after Renaissance writer Christine de Pizan, Marie de Gournay threw herself into the *querelle des femmes* debate. Enough exaggeration, be it women's excellence or women's inferiority, Gournay thinks and claims that she is content to establish the *equality* of men and women. Women and men are more equal than different, and many women are more different amongst themselves than some women are from men.

Gournay's role as an important feminist forerunner is very much a discovery of recent scholarship, and a discovery still in process.[9] This illustrates how the history of feminism is not linear, but characterized by rupture, forgetting and re-discovering.

Born in Paris in 1565 to a family of minor nobility, Marie le Jars was the first of six children. A few years after her birth her father bought the estate of Gournay-sur-Aronde in Picardy and the title that went with it, and the le Jars family moved from Paris, taking on the name de Gournay. Marie was given limited education but managed to educate herself. For example, she taught herself Latin by comparing original texts with French translations. She studied the classics and Greek philosophy and is reported to have been particularly familiar with Plato. When she was 18 she discovered the *Essays* of Michel de Montaigne, which were to have a decisive influence on her. Gournay sent Montaigne a letter encouraging him to visit the Gournay family and after meeting in Paris they developed a warm friendship. Montaigne was 32 years her senior and called her his *fille d'alliance*, his adopted daughter.

After Montaigne died, his widow commissioned Gournay to edit a new edition of his essays. She thus edited the third edition of Montaigne's *Essays*, the 1595 edition published with a *Preface* defending

Montaigne against his critics. It is primarily for this role and work as Montaigne's editor that has given her a certain reputation.[10] Gournay's friendship with Montaigne was decisive in many ways for her; it probably infused her ambitions of making a life for herself as a *femme de lettre* instead of marrying, a quite exceptional choice for a woman, particularly a woman of her social rank. Montaigne also gave her several important acquaintances and probably opened some doors that would otherwise have been closed to her.

It is also impossible not to ask whether her idea of equality owes debt to Montaigne. No wonder perhaps that Gournay was excited about Montaigne's essays as he must also be called a forerunner of feminism. In *Essays*, Book III, he writes: "Women are not entirely wrong when they reject the moral rules proclaimed in society, since it is we men alone who have made them" (Montaigne, 2003: 964). Montaigne also criticizes the double moral standard within sexual morality. It is expected of women to be cold and warm at the same time, equally chaste and willing, Montaigne writes, as he concludes that "I say male and female are cast in the same mould: save for education and custom the difference between them is not great" (ibid., 1016).

When Montaigne sees sexual difference as grounded on upbringing, education and accepted practice, we are perhaps catching sight of an early version of an argument for gender as a cultural construction. The claim that men and women were made in the same mould might be the forerunner of Gournay's idea of equality. And as a development of Montaigne she suggests altering the upbringing of women by offering them education.

Gournay's pamphlet *The Equality of Men and Women* suffered (like many women's writings) complete oblivion after her lifetime and wasn't reprinted until 1910 (Hillman in Gournay, 2002: 17). She did not, however, write in a complete vacuum; as we shall see later the learned Anna Maria van Schurman (1607–1678) was an enthusiastic reader of Gournay. Between the 17th and 19th centuries Gournay was forgotten and her feminist and egalitarian views with her. One can only speculate on the reasons for such oblivion, but the fact that she was the victim of much ridicule and mockery in her old age did certainly little to secure her respect and reputation.

Gournay's method

Gournay's method is worth a few words. After having presented her opinion, that women are neither better nor worse than men but equal, she provides an impressive list of names as evidence for her case. She begins by listing famous women from Antiquity to her own day before turning to interpretations of the Scripture. This listing of famous women from history is a "tradition" going back to Italian Renaissance writer Giovanni Bocaccio's *Famous Women* (*De mulieribus claris*) of 1362. Bocaccio's work is the first collection of biographies in Western literature devoted exclusively to women. Bocaccio's *Famous Women* inspired a wave of catalogues of great women.[11] After having reminded her readers that Plato had suggested including women in the organization of the Republic, she begins her listing of great women by referring to Hypatia from Alexandria – this city only second to Rome in Antiquity and once ruled by a woman, as Gournay says. Her list of famous names also demonstrates her knowledge of classical literature. Among the women she lists are Hypatia, Themistoclea (Pythagoras' teacher), Diotima, Aspasia, Cornelia (mother of Tiberius and Gaius), Laelia (daughter of Caius Laelius Sapiens) and in her 1634 edition she also adds Anna Maria van Schurman.

This "practice" of giving examples of great women as an argument against the subordination of women is one also practiced by other feminist writers such as Christine de Pizan, Anna Maria van Schurman, Ludvig Holberg and Simone de Beauvoir. Gournay's *Equality* is dedicated to queen Anne (of Austria), married to the French King Louis XIII (and mother of Louis XIV). In her dedication, Gournay boldly insists that the queen educate herself so as to set an example to others: "you will serve as a mirror for your sex … if you deign to raise yourself to the degree of merit and perfection that I propose to you by the aid of those great books" (Gournay, 2002: 74). The function of exemplarity or the use of female examples reaches in the case of Gournay an epistemological status. These examples do not only function as proper models after which to pattern one's life but constitutes Gournay's *method*, so to say. She makes her case for gender equality based on the exemplarity of great women from the past as they are proof of women's capacity to perform more than sewing and cooking. She complains on the first page that, as a rule, women are confined to the distaff, to the distaff alone. Her many examples of learned women have the function of reversing this. In fact, the examples are her argument, or her "testimonies" or "witness" as she calls them (ibid., 85).

Through her listing of famous names, men as well as women, she demonstrates her knowledge of classics. She refers to Plato's *Republic* and the wise Diotima of *Symposium*. Diotima is the hidden female voice, Socrates' teacher of the meaning of love in Plato's famous drinking party, *The Symposium*. Why would Plato/Socrates give such an important role to a woman if he/they thought women inferior to men, Gournay asks rhetorically. Which is more or the less the same question asked by Luce

Irigaray in her text "Sorcerer Love: A Reading of Plato, *Symposium*, 'Diotima's Speech'" from 1984. For Irigaray the point is that Diotima does not have a position as either/or, but in between. Diotima is neither present nor absent, neither subject nor object. Diotima represents sameness and difference, she is equal but different. Diotima as a figure of the woman intellectual has been a crucial role model and example for female thinkers. An important point regarding the difference between Plato's assessment of women in his *Republic* and Gournay's own assessment of women is her use of the concept *equality*.

Yet another method applied by Gournay is the *reductio ad absurdum*. Gournay's text is also a wonderful piece of irony at times. Already on the second page, after having presented the debate, she says: "Amid the chirping of their lofty conversation, hark how such intellects compare the two sexes: in their opinion, the supreme excellence women may achieve is to resemble ordinary men" (Gournay, 2002: 76). She here makes fun of men who overrate and glorify themselves. The text ends with a discussion of the Scripture. Humans were created male and female, they were created as one, as equal and not hierarchal, thus "if man is more than women then woman is more than man". The only difference between men and women is women's reproductive capacities that men somehow seem to rob: "Jesus Christ is called Son of Man, although he is that only of a woman" (ibid., 87). Gournay ends her text with a *reductio ad absurdum* argument. If we suppose that the Scripture commanded women to submit to man, and that she was unworthy of opposing him, then this absurdity would follow:

> Woman would find herself worthy of having been made in the image of the Creator, worthy of the holy Eucharist, of the mysteries of the redemption, of paradise, and of the sight – indeed the possession – of God, yet not of the advantages and privileges of man. Would this not declare man to be more precious and more exalted than all these things, and hence commit the gravest of blasphemies?
>
> (ibid., 95)

Men are not only overrating themselves and placing themselves over women, but in doing so they also raise themselves over God.

Contemporary philosopher Eileen O'Neill argues that there are certain problems with regarding Gournay's thesis as a piece of philosophy, since Gournay (according to O'Neill) explicitly rejects the use of arguments. In her article "Justifying the Inclusion of Women in Our Histories of Philosophy" (2007), O'Neill claims that Gournay's method is rooted in Pyrrhonean scepticism. On this reading Gournay is voicing Pyrrhonean doubts about reason's ability to assent in the face of equipollent arguments. According to O'Neill, then, the philosophical importance of Gournay and her *Equality* pamphlet lies in the fact that she raises the level of discussion in *querelle des femmes* to a point where the gender issue is recognizably philosophical.

O'Neill also writes: "In fact, to my knowledge this is the very first early modern philosophical text published by a woman" (O'Neill, 2007: 35). Although the aim of this book is to trace the origin and history of feminist thought, we also visit the history of women thinkers. It is inevitable not to notice that most women thinkers of all ages have been interested in issues of gender while on the other hand issues of gender have for the most part not been accepted as philosophy proper. To include women in the canon of philosophy, then, we must first admit that questions of gender are also philosophical questions. The core of philosophical questioning can be reduced to the questions: who am I, and how have I become who I am? In her book *Undoing Gender* Judith Butler discusses transsexual subjectivity, but her questions might just as well be posed from the point of view of being a woman:

> Who can I become in a world where the meanings and limits of the subject are set out in advance for me? By what norms am I constrained as I begin to become that for which there is no place within the given regime of truth?
>
> (Butler, 2004: 58)

These questions are just as relevant for a woman of the 17th century as for a transgender person of the 21st and illustrate how there is nothing like a neutral or gender-neutral being. The answer to the question "Who am I?" necessarily involves gender.

Montaigne, equality and modern subjectivity

The literature on Descartes often speaks about a possible influence from Montaigne; the *Essays* make the case for "experience" as a source of knowledge, which again leads to a sort of autobiographical subjective reasoning where the text is individualized by a first-person perspective. Interestingly, in her text *The Equality of Men and Women*, as well as in "Apology for the Woman Writing", Gournay also makes use of first-person perspective. If we interpret this subjective narrative as a manifestation of her gender, an expression of "I am a woman", this places Gournay in the company of other pioneering feminists such as Mary Wollstonecraft and Simone de Beauvoir. Professor of literature and Beauvoir scholar Toril

Philosophies of equality 35

Moi argues that the use of first-person singular is a significant stylistic feature of Simone de Beauvoir and claims in her essay "I Am a Woman" (Moi, 2001) that there is a close connection between the personal and the philosophical in Beauvoir's *The Second Sex*. Only the study of concrete situations and experiences will tell us what a woman is, Moi claims, hence Beauvoir's subjectivity is always present in the text. Thus, it is not through metaphysical speculation, Moi continues, but through analyses of expressions and anecdotes from everyday life that Beauvoir arrives at the claim that woman is the Other (ibid., 171). Moi makes the point that "I" is the very first word in Beauvoir's text: "I hesitated a long time before writing a book on woman". In this, way according to Moi, Beauvoir introduces herself "firmly yet unobtrusively as the author of her own text" (ibid., 172). Moi compares Beauvoir's introduction to the introduction of another influential feminist text, Luce Irigaray's *Speculum of the Other Woman* where Irigaray (according to Moi) does not assert her own subjectivity, but masks her voice (ibid., 174).

The main point I want to make is that Beauvoir is not unique, as Moi suggests, in introducing a subjective voice. Also, Mary Wollstonecraft uses the personal pronoun "I" in the very first sentence of *A Vindication of the Rights of Woman* (1792) and Virginia Woolf presents her "I" already in the second sentence of "A Room of One's Own" (1929). To borrow Moi's reading of Beauvoir, it is possible to argue then that also Marie le Jars de Gournay – firmly yet unobtrusively – introduces herself as the author of her own text by her use of an autobiographical voice. It is not unthinkable that Beauvoir shares Gournay and Descartes' inspiration and influence from Montaigne. Montaigne's project of self-exploration with the aim of discovering a universal human nature agrees with Descartes and Gournay as well as Beauvoir and her many philosophical and literary autobiographies.

At least we can reaffirm that Marie de Gournay shares the autobiographical voice with Montaigne and Descartes, which she also shares with Wollstonecraft, Woolf and Beauvoir (the negative flipside of this individualized subjective focus is, for women, slander and gossip, which all four women were victims of; this is also Irigaray's explicit reason for not sharing any personal and private information about herself).

It is common to designate the subject of Modernity as the Cartesian subject and likewise the Cartesian ego as the foundation of modern philosophy. *The Meditations* as well as *Discourse on the Method* are both written in a first-person perspective. As we know, the Cartesian subject is situating itself in an episteme of modern scientificity, the "I think" (the *cogito*) is the foundation/basis and guarantee for scientific truth. We can detect a common influence from Montaigne in Descartes as well as in Gournay. Montaigne has been read as the predecessor of Descartes and situated in the history of the constitution of the Western subject (Melehy, 1997). According to Hassan Melehy, Montaigne was the "first" to use the first-person singular pronoun to represent the autonomous writing subject. What I would like to bring to light is that also Marie de Gournay writes from the first-person perspective. Within different versions of feminism, the first-person perspective is given different accounts. Literary critic Susan S. Lanser (Lanser, 1992) suggests that Charlotte Brontë's *Jane Eyre* of 1847 marks the imposition of a self-authorized female voice. Lanser points to the fact that Jane Eyre's initials spell J.E., "je", French for "I", and while it is obviously true that *Jane Eyre* is an important contribution to the development of female subjectivity in literature, my point is that it is even more striking that Marie de Gournay gave herself the authority to speak and write in a first-person language already in the 17th century. If Gournay's subjective voice is indebted to Montaigne, in the same way that Melehy claims that Descartes is, then here is a link between Descartes and Gournay. A twofold link; influence from Montaigne, and writings in a first-person perspective. This again shows how feminism is not situated in the margins of European culture, but right at the heart of it. Montaigne initiated an understanding of subjectivity that in the hands of Descartes and Gournay fostered a notion of self that has been influential ever since, and culminated in Kantian autonomy, the so-called Kantian "Copernican revolution".

From the point of view of intellectual history, it is worth mentioning that the centralizing of the subject in philosophy and thought parallels the development of the central perspective and centralizing of the subject in visual art. The central perspective, invented and developed by Filippo Brunelleschi in 15th century Italy, is a powerful depth illusion governed by a single vanishing point. The central perspective places the subject, the viewer, as the very centre of the artwork.

In Gournay's *Equality* pamphlet she quite courageously presented her opinions to the public. After having established in the introductory words that there is an on-going debate concerning the status of women, she boldly expresses her own views on the matter using a first-person perspective. Concerning the question of what kind of equality Gournay was aiming for, we must allow her not to answer the 21st century standard or understanding of equality. Her demand for equality concerns equality between men and women only, she did not e.g. question the French absolute monarchy, but argued against the Salic laws that prevented women from inheriting the throne. The throne or monarchy itself, however, is never questioned by Gournay. Being of minor nobility herself she seems never to have any doubts about the social system in 17th century France. Her understanding of equality becomes clearer in the second part of the pamphlet where she says: "the human animal, taken rightly, is neither man nor woman, the sexes having been made double, not so as to constitute a difference in species, but for the sake of propagation alone" (Gournay, 2002: 86). Man and woman are thus equal, only differentiated by their reproductive capacities, which is not a difference in either mental or moral capacities. The difference that can be observed between men and women, Gournay claims, is due to women's lack of good education (ibid., 81). Thus, we can conclude that Gournay's demand for gender equality goes against the Aristotelian understanding of women as subordinated by nature, rather claiming that sexual difference is culturally produced. The core of her argument is thus very close and related to Simone de Beauvoir's famous dictum from *The Second Sex*: "One is not born, but rather becomes, woman". Femininity is culturally constructed rather than a natural state, and Gournay's contribution can be seen in the light of what we today consider the nature/nurture debate.

Education as a road to equality

Right at the beginning of *A Vindication of the Rights of Woman,* Mary Wollstonecraft (1759–1797) identifies the problem of gender inequality as the lack of education given to women: "the neglect of education of my fellow-creatures is the grand source of the misery" (Wollstonecraft, 1995: 74). The importance of education for equality between men and women runs like a "leit-motif" through Wollstonecraft's *Vindication*. Education was also a primary concern for Wollstonecraft in her first book *Thoughts on the Education of Daughters*, where she writes that she wants to teach girls to think. Education for women as a way of improving their status was an issue occupying feminists throughout the Early Modern period. Traditional justification for the denial of rights to women was based on the claim that women were not capable of reason, which was seen as a criterion for holders of rights at the time. Early Modern female philosophers thus aimed to show that women had no less capacity for reason. Their arguments draw on the idea that apparent differences in rationality were the effects of differences in education and socialization.

Venetian-born Christine de Pizan (1363–1430) suggested in her *The Book of the City of Ladies* that education would make women more equal to men. The book is a thought experiment about a city where women are appreciated and defended. The book was not translated into English until 1982, which again illustrates the lack of any continuous and coherent historic consciousness about the early origins of feminist thought. Pizan opens the book by asking how it is possible that so many men, even educated men, can speak so negatively about women. Can they possibly be wrong, can possibly even Aristotle who thought that a woman was an incomplete man, be wrong? In company of the later Wollstonecraft and Beauvoir, Pizan traces the source of women's inferiority to their lack of education. Had it been customary to send one's daughters to school and methodically teach them science in the same way as one does with sons, girls would understand the beautiful arts and science just like boys. According to Pizan, then, there is nothing in women's nature that makes them inferior, it's their lack of education.

For Marie de Gournay as well, education was a point of departure for discussing equality. According to her, the supposed gap between the minds of men and women was due to a gap in training, an "abundance of outright and blatantly bad education". She asks: "is there more difference between them [women] and men than among themselves – according to the training they receive, according to whether they are brought up in a city or a village or according to nationality?" (Gournay, 2002: 81). English and French women exceed Italian women in dealing with the world, she continues, and rhetorically ask if this is so due to the nature of Italian ladies or if it is because French and English women have fewer restrictions than the Italians.

Female education was also a focus elsewhere in Europe. In 1650 the remarkable Dutch *femme savante* (learned lady) Anna Maria van Schurman (1607–1678) published the short text: "Whether the study of letters is fitting for a Christian woman". Protestant insistence that everyone should be able to read the Bible led to an increasingly literate society. Rejections of clerical hierarchism paralleled rejection of clerical domination of education. In search of a purer Christianity, proponents wanted to read the Bible and Christian writers afresh without the previously dominating intellectual framework of medieval Scholasticism. Schurman wanted to extend this to women, i.e. Christian women. Schurman was famous for her intellectual abilities. She corresponded with Europe's leading intellectuals and even met with René Descartes. She also knew the writings of Marie de Gournay and wrote a short poem honouring Gournay, which illustrates that these Early Modern women did not write in a vacuum but that there were some connections between them.[12]

> Anna Maria van Schurman congratulates
> the great and noble-minded heroine of Gournay
> strong defender of the cause of our sex.

> You bear the arms of Pallas, bold heroine in battles
> And so that you may carry the laurels, you bear the arms of Pallas.
> Thus it is fitting for you to make a defense for the innocent sex
> And turn the weapons of harmful men against them.
> Lead on, glory of Gournay, we shall follow your standard,
> For in you our cause advances, which is mightier than strength.[13]

Of Schurman, Gournay reciprocated on her side again and wrote when she listed learned women as examples for her cause:

> But then if Tycho Brahe, the famous astronomer and Danish baron, had lived in our day, would he not have celebrated that new star recently discovered in his region – let us call her thus – Mademoiselle van Schurman, the rival of those illustrious ladies in eloquence, and of their lyric poets too, even in their own Latin language, and who, besides that language, possesses all the others, ancient and modern, and all the liberal arts?
>
> (Gournay, 2002: 78)

Schurman's own defense of women's education is fundamentally theological. The issue for Schurman is not whether *all* women ought to be educated, but whether *Christian* women ought to study. She argues that the study of letters is "able to move us to easier and fuller knowledge of Sacred Scripture", which in her view is the purpose of education. Her arguments are organized as an exercise in logic and syllogisms, and one of them has certain affinities with Wollstonecraft's arguments. Action is better than inaction, Schurman claims, and adds that doing nothing has worse consequences than e.g. the study of letters. Also, Wollstonecraft claims that the poor education of women leads to degradation and stupidity, which again is harmful to society. It seems they are both aiming at a rhetoric saying that if we have to choose between uneducated and potentially harmful women, and educated women who either contribute to improved faith or in the case of Wollstonecraft the improvement of society, then it must be quite obvious what to choose. Although Schurman develops her opinion within a religious framework, the core of her argument is secular. Justification of her argument is not sought within theology but what she aims at is a benefit principle; she wants to give women education in order to make themselves useful. These are ideas we can still recognize and respond to. Although Eve is responsible for the Fall, for bringing sin into the world by eating the forbidden apple, this does not prevent Schurman from arguing that it would be an advantage for all if women could study the Bible.

It has been pointed out elsewhere that Protestantism plays a significant role in the history of feminism, e.g. Julia Kristeva's "Women's Time" (1986). For Kristeva, it is Protestantism's loss of the Virgin Mary as a female model that initiates a female dissatisfaction that eventually leads to modern feminism. With Schurman close at hand we see that Protestantism's urge to individual and personal relations to the Scripture, and the consequential quest for education of women, is Protestantism's primary contribution to feminism. Although the lack of female images might be a psychological explanation for the rise of feminism, demands for education of women as an expansion of human equality are an ethical issue, and as such a philosophical one. While Catholicism offered a life in convents for women with intellectual talents, this was no longer a possibility for Protestant women; they had to find other loopholes to argue in favour of letting them learn to read and write.

As did the Englishwoman Mary Astell (1666–1731) who in 1694 proposed an academy for Protestant ladies equivalent to a convent, where unmarried women could devote themselves to religious studies and other concerns. This proposal was published in the pamphlet *A Serious Proposal for the Ladies, for the Advancement of their True and Greatest Interest*, with the subtitle *By a Lover of her Sex*. Astell finds that there is something amiss in ladies: their enthusiasm for fashion and beauty ought rather to be spent on serious reflection on their minds (Astell, 2002: 52). Women's inferiority is not due to nature but to lack of *education*:

> So that instead of inquiring why all Women are not wise and good, we have reason to wonder that there are any so. Were the Men as much neglected, and as little care taken to cultivate and improve them, perhaps they wou'd be far from surpassing those whom they now dispise, that they themselves wou'd sink into the greatest stupidity and brutality.
> (ibid., 57)

Equal education of men and women would bring about equally wise and stupid men and women. What stops women from seeking education is the false imperative that it is enough for a woman to care about her dress and appearances:

> When a poor Young Lady is taught to value her self on nothing but her Cloaths, and to think she is very fine when well accoutred. When she hears say that 'tis Wisdom is enough for her to know to dress, that she may become amiable in his eyes [...]
> (ibid., 69)

then she cannot be blamed for this misinformation.

A quest for female education was likewise called for by contemporary of Mary Astell, lady Damaris Masham (1658–1708). Masham was one of the earliest English female philosophers and a close friend of John Locke. She was also the daughter of Cambridge Platonist Ralph Cudworth. Her writings are a mix of Platonism, Lockean ideas and her own feminist viewpoints. Masham's argument in *Occasional Thoughts in reference to a Vertuous or Christian Life* of 1705 for giving women education was that since it is women who take care of upbringing of children and prepare them for the outside world, and instruct them in the Christian faith, this is better done by someone who is not ignorant of the world. It is a mother's duty, she writes, to form the minds of children so that they become wise and virtuous men and women. To perform this task, they need knowledge:

> For it cannot be deny'd that this Knowledge would hereafter be more or less useful to Ladies, in inabling them either themselves to teach their Children, or better to over-see and direct those who do so.
>
> (Masham, 1705: 90)

The world would be a better place if women were educated, Masham argued. Her argument anticipates the later Mary Wollstonecraft who also points to the responsibility of mothers.

Almost a hundred years after Mary Astell and Damaris Masham, Wollstonecraft observes that women are still kept in ignorance and taught to be fools preoccupied with dresses and their own appearances. According to her, women are kept in ignorance under the specious name of "innocence", i.e. they are being kept in a state of childhood (Wollstonecraft, 1995: 87–88). She writes:

> Where is then the sexual difference, when the education has been the same? All the differences that I can discern, arises from the superior advantage of liberty, which enables the former to see more of life.
>
> (ibid., 92)

Women are neither given information nor education and experiences are kept from them; they are not allowed to grow into responsible grownups like men but rather formed to be dependent on them, Wollstonecraft thinks. Men complain about the follies and vices of women, she writes, while at the same time it is men who insist they behave like children and it is only in men's interests to keep them that way. Men have a double standard regarding women, Wollstonecraft claims; they are taught to please men, but it is about time they are taught to please themselves. The focus on beauty and appearances makes woman into "being-for-another", to borrow the language of Beauvoir. Wollstonecraft calls for "a revolution in female manners", she claims that it is time to "restore them to their lost dignity" so that they can contribute to "reform the world" (ibid., 117). Wollstonecraft again anticipates Beauvoir's thoughts that a woman ought to be a "being-for-herself", as well as Luce Irigaray's insistence that woman in Western culture is only a mirroring of man's desires and fantasies, a thought already articulated by Montaigne. Wollstonecraft strongly advocates that education is the solution to the inequality between the sexes. Education of women will bring equality to women and secure them the same rights as men.

Mary Wollstonecraft brings the equality debate one step further by saying that she will discuss education for women of all classes. So far, discussions of education for women have related to upper class women and ladies. A further discussion of Wollstonecraft will follow in Chapter 4.

In Simone de Beauvoir's *The Second Sex* as well we find that women are encouraged to take upon education as a road to equality. Beauvoir and Wollstonecraft alike insist that women take responsibility for their own situation. It is unfortunate that they have been kept in ignorance, or in "immanence", as Beauvoir put it, but nothing will happen until women take it in their own hands to change the direction. Women have been treated as though they were secondary, like children, beings or mirrors of men's fantasies. To escape this situation women must take responsibility for their own fate and situation. Enough passivity and immanence. In order to achieve equal status and rights, women must behave like proactive responsible individuals.

The focal point of this chapter has been the philosophical history of equality, by presenting Marie de Gournay, who was the very first thinker we know of to propose that men and women might be equal. Although the main aim of this book is to trace the origin and history of feminist thought, this history is intertwined with the history of women thinkers.

Notes

1 See: https://www.un.org/sustainabledevelopment/sustainable-development-goals
2 Joan Kelly dates the *querelle des femmes* from 1400 to 1789.

3 I.e. *Disputation nova contra mulieres, qua probatur eas hominess non esse*, published anonymously in 1595.
4 Historian Cissie Fairchilds traces the origin of the idea of women as sinful to the early church fathers, who found it very difficult to live in celibacy. To them (Fairchilds claims) every woman was a sexual temptress, a lure to sin (Fairchilds, 2007: 11).
5 See Martinich, Allhof & Vaidya: *Early Modern Philosophy: Essential Readings with Commentary.* "General Introduction" by A. P. Martinich. Blackwell Publishing, Malden, Oxford, Victoria, 2007.
6 See Florian Cajori: *A History of Mathematical Notations.* Dover Publications, Inc., New York, 1993: "In printed books before Recorde, equality was usually expressed rhetorically by such words as *aequales, aequatur, esgale, faciunt, ghelijck,* or *gleich,* and sometimes by the abbreviated form *aeq.*"
7 I have to date not been able to find any literature that reflects upon the relation between the invention of the equals sign and the development of equality as a political term.
8 Historians of philosophy Jacqueline Broad and Karen Green also claim in *A History of Women's Political Thought in Europe* (2002) that Gournay was "the first to propose the equality of men and women" (125).
9 See e.g. Richard Hillman's "Introduction" to English translation of Marie de Gournay.
10 For a thorough biography on Gournay, see: Marjory Henry Ilsley: *A Daughter of the Renaissance: Marie le Jars de Gournay: Her Life and Works.* Mouton & Co. The Hague, 1963.
11 Among which were Filippo da Bergamo's *Of Illustrious Women*, Pierre de Brantôme's *Lives of Illustrious Women,* Pierre Le Moynes' *Gallerie of Heroic Women,* and Pietro Paolo de Riberas' *Immortal Triumphs and Heroic Enterprises of 845 Women.* See Virginia Brown: "Introduction" to Giovanni Bocaccio: *Famous Women.* The I Tatti Renaissance Library, Harvard University Press, Cambridge, Massachusetts, London, England, 2001.
12 Siep Stuurman and Tjitske Akkerman (1998) argue against the view that we only have scattered remains and traces of early feminism by claiming that such inter-textuality shows that there *is* a European feminist tradition. The problem is rather that this tradition is underestimated and forgotten.
13 Ibid., 13.

3 Cartesian feminism

Interpretations of Descartes

While many contemporary feminists interpret Cartesian philosophy as the origin of male domination in philosophy, women of Early Modern Europe saw Cartesianism as extremely liberating. This chapter explores the spreading consequences of Descartes' philosophy for feminist thought, with a special look at François Poulain de la Barre (1647–1723), who developed Cartesian thinking into a feminist framework.

From the late 20th century, René Descartes (1596–1650) has been a target of feminist criticism, according to which Descartes' work is responsible for the common association of reason with maleness. Feminist philosophers like Susan Bordo and Genvieve Lloyd both see Descartes as liable for the alleged maleness of philosophical ideals of reason. Lloyd claims in her influential *The Man of Reason* that Descartes' thinking sparked a metaphorical association between masculinity and reason on the one hand and irrationality, emotions and femininity, on the other (Lloyd, 1984). Lloyd also argues that Cartesian dualism is particularly problematic for feminism. Reflecting on feminism's relationship with Cartesian philosophy in 2002, she writes:

> What made the Cartesian philosophy suspect for feminists was its association with the doctrine of dualism – the rigid separation of minds and bodies as utterly distinct kinds of being. The dichotomy came to be seen as reinforcing the denigration of women, in association with body, in opposition to an ideal of reason associated with "male" transcendence.
>
> (Lloyd, 2002)

Considering the early reception of Descartes in a historical perspective presents a very different picture of Cartesianism. Rather than seeing

Cartesianism as masculinisation of thought, Early Modern feminist thinkers saw Cartesianism as making openings for women, even providing women with possibilities they had never had before. The Cartesian claim that reason is the most equally distributed sense among men, together with an "egalitarian" epistemology, according to which knowledge is accessible to everyone, gave women a possibility of taking part in a public philosophical dialogue that was new to them.

For contemporary feminists' criticism of Descartes, it is his dualism, the mind-body split that is the count of indictment. In Descartes' own days the separation of mind and body was in fact seen as a favourable doctrine for women, since the mind by this account has no sex. Descartes' methodological doubt had led him to an unshakable certainty anchored in the *cogito*. The thinking subject or the mind was constituted and given priority over the body. Hence the physical difference was only secondary and the mental equality more significant. The mind-body dualism brought about a possibility of arguing that while the body is sexually differentiated, the mind is sexless. Hence women have the same intellectual capabilities as men and ought therefore to be given the same possibilities for education and participation in civil society. Dualism or the mind-body problem was, however, not introduced to philosophy by Descartes. The relationship between mental and physical properties had already been discussed by Plato and his theory of forms, where the soul is not dependent on the body.

Since the Renaissance, new discoveries and new scientific achievements had challenged the authority of tradition. Modernity represents in many ways a break with tradition and the past. Assumptions and customs of the past can no longer constitute bases for opinions and practices. These must seek legitimation and regulation through observation and rational self-reflection. Science no longer looks for Aristotelic or Platonic forms but has to search for mechanistic explanations. The new science departed from customary notions and saw the world in a completely new way, e.g. Copernicus' heliocentric theory, according to which the sun is the centre of the solar system and that the planets circle the sun, which was later confirmed by Johannes Kepler and Galileo Galilei. Descartes' philosophy is a consequence of and an answer to problems generated by the new science. In the introduction to *Discours de la Methode* he claims that there are certain topics that are more adequately answered through the help of philosophy than by theology (the existence of God and the immortality of the soul). The most important legacy of Descartes is the introduction of scientific *method* as the best way to reliable knowledge and truth. The essence of Descartes' philosophy is to let reason and rationality constitute our guidelines rather than dogma and tradition.

Cartesiomania

René Descartes, "the father of modern philosophy" (a description already used by Voltaire and Locke), was a source of inspiration even in his own days. The success and discoveries of the natural sciences prompted current questions about certainty; how can we know anything for certain? Disappointed with the philosophy and theology of his day, Descartes proposed a model for human knowledge built on mathematical reasoning. For Descartes, mathematics offered the exemplary certainty and clarity that he hoped could be achieved in other areas. Descartes advocated a new scientific method grounded in observation to replace dogmatic Scholasticism, where science is deducted from first principles. "Method" has ever since been understood as the recipe or procedure for deciding what is true. Methodological doubt led Descartes to the certainty of his own existence. According to him, there had to be a conscious subject doubting, which led him to the famous *cogito ergo sum* (I think therefore I am). In his works *Discourse* (short for *Discourse on the Method*) and *Meditations* (short for *Meditations on the First Philosophy*) he is trying to explain his discoveries and methods to a wide public. *Discourse* is written in the vernacular so that women and uneducated people could also read it. It is also written in the first person and in a relatively accessible language. Reading Descartes' philosophy did not require either philosophical or scientific training; in fact, it was addressed to those without formal training.

Descartes worked on arithmetic, algebra and geometry, believing that mathematics possessed a kind of precision and certainty that traditional philosophy lacked. In Descartes' view, mathematics was the paradigm and model for all human understanding.

Descartes begins the *Discourse* by claiming that good sense is the most evenly distributed thing in the world and continues in the second paragraph: "For myself, I have never presumed my mind to be any way more accomplished than that of the common man" (Descartes, 1996: 5). No surprise that this text appealed to an uneducated audience. While presenting his method he says that his aim is not to teach a method that everyone should follow, but that his only ambition is to show how he has conducted his method. He admits the possibility of being wrong and says that it is possible that he might be "mistaking bits of copper and glass for gold and diamonds" (ibid., 6). He continues by telling that through studying, reading and travelling "I learned not to believe too firmly in anything that only example and custom had persuaded me of" (ibid., 11). In addition to elements like the language and the accessibility, the content of Descartes' philosophy plays a major role for a feminist account and/or appropriation. One's own experience is according to Descartes more trustworthy than custom, habit and received wisdom. "To rid oneself of all the opinions one has hitherto accepted" (ibid., 15) can naturally lead to viewing the sexes and the relation between the sexes in a completely new way. This Cartesian epistemology was a source of inspiration for feminists like Poulain de la Barre and Mary Astell, as we shall see.

The method itself is also simple and open to anyone, which is why it is referred to as "Descartes' egalitarian epistemology". It is a scientific method that can be applied by anyone, anywhere, and at any time. It is a method of simple, clear-headed and rational inquiry, which all people can apply if they clear their minds of prejudice. No special training is needed, no religious discipline, no knowledge of texts or of history is necessary. As British philosopher Bernard Williams points out, Descartes' *Meditations* is an exercise in thinking rather than a treatise. It is presented as an encouragement and guide to readers who will think philosophically themselves (Williams, 1996). This explains some of the popularity of Descartes, particularly among women and early feminists.

Descartes's epistemology (or "first philosophy") is his theory of what needs to be known for stable and exact sciences to be possible at all. Descartes is searching for "foundations" of knowledge through methodical doubt. Methodical doubt is a way of searching for certainty by systematically doubting everything. By doubting everything, one will find some indubitable certainties. In this view, doubt provides foundations for knowledge because it helps eliminate error.

While scepticism was nothing new, Descartes' use of it was. His rebuttal of scepticism depends on the existence of a God who has created us and is "no deceiver"; God will not allow us to be systematically mistaken.

Having subtracted God from the study of the natural sciences, Descartes was accused of heresy and blasphemy and accused of denying original sin. *Meditations* was placed on the Index of Forbidden Books by the Roman Catholic Church in 1663 and condemned by the Jesuits the same year. The inquisitors were particularly sensitive to books that were accessible to the uneducated public, and all of Descartes' works ended up on the Index. His philosophy was thought to be dangerous for Christian faith and conservative forces were offended by the anti-Scholasticism of his writings. Some also feared that the methodological doubt would open or legalize completely freethinking.[1] A long series of prohibitions culminated in a French royal ban on teaching Cartesian philosophy in 1691.

Why then would Descartes be interesting for 17th century feminists? There are at least three elements of his thinking that have received attention by feminists: (1) his critique of the authority of tradition, (2) his epistemological and moral egalitarianism and (3) his theories of the mind and body. All three points open for certain possibilities taken up by his feminist followers.

Cartesianism, women and salons

Although Descartes today is regarded as the "father of modern philosophy" and his writings are mandatory for most studies of modern philosophy, his popularity was not an immediate success and breakthrough. As pointed out above, universities banned his writings and the Catholic Church placed his books on the Index. The salons, however, were not under the royal ban on Cartesian philosophy.

The dissemination and discussion of Descartes' thinking was facilitated by the salons run by intellectual upper-class women. The salon culture was a decisive factor in the spreading of Enlightenment thinking. From a feminist perspective the salon culture is intriguing because it was initiated and run by women as well as a site that offered some possibilities for women with intellectual talent and capacities.

The women Cartesians, or *cartésiennes* as they were called, were comparatively quite numerous, but we barely hear about them in the standard works on the history of philosophy. The reason why these women have disappeared out of history is complex, one obvious reason being that few of them published anything. They left few traces of concrete text-material. Even Madame de Bonnevaux, who reportedly lectured over Descartes in her salon, did not leave anything written (Harth, 1992). The few who actually wrote something published anonymously and were more interested in religious questions about faith and revelation, a genre with minimal historical interest and which has gone out of philosophy. The *cartésiennes* didn't write on epistemology, science and truth, the topics that have become central within philosophy. The lack of written texts can also be explained by pointing to the most important form of communication within the salon: conversation. Texts were interpreted and discussed primarily orally, and not in writing.

What has survived as written testimony of some of these women is their correspondence, like Madame de Sévigné's letters to her daughter, published in 1726, and Princess Elisabeth of Bohemia's correspondence with Descartes (where she challenges his division between mind and body). It can also be argued that our relationship to text and writing has changed since the days of *les cartésiennes*. The genius aesthetics of German idealism and English romanticism have forever changed our understanding of a written text. Ever since Immanuel Kant's *Critique of Judgement*, a text is understood as the expression of one individual ingenious subject's thinking. Salon-aesthetics, if we can use such a term, implies a rather more collective attitude towards the creation of texts, more in the lines of a kind of "Gesamtkunstwerk". The famous master of maxim La Rochefoucauld (1613–1680) circulated drafts of his maxims in the salons including comments and feedback in the final version, which then actually had *several* authors. The absence of texts by *les cartésiennes* can also be explained by the 17th century ideal of female manners. Many women regarded their role primarily as contributing inspiration and help for male thinking. It is not unlikely that Diotima's role as "midwife" for Socrates' thinking in *Symposion* was an important ideal for female intellectuals. The point I want to make is that the salon functioned as a *catalyst* for Descartes' philosophy. Even if salon women did not write and publish on Descartes' philosophy, they contributed considerably to the dissemination and spreading of his thinking.

If we jump a bit in time, to approximately a century later, women in England had managed to find a literary voice, publishing novels and pamphlets. In Mary Hays' novel of 1759, *Memoirs of Emma Courtney*, we find a possible statement of how the encounter with Descartes' writings might have been for women. Written in the decade following the French Revolution, Hays' novel is partly autobiographical and is based on Hays' own struggle with romance and Enlightenment philosophy:

> [M]y mind began to be emancipated, doubts had been suggested to it, I reasoned freely, endeavoured to arrange and methodize my opinions, and to trace them fearlessly through all their consequences: while from exercising my thoughts with freedom, I seemed to acquire new strength and dignity of character. I met with some of the writings of Descartes and was seized with a passion for metaphysical enquiries. I began to think about the nature of the soul – whether it was a composition of the elements, the result of organized matter, or a subtle and ethereal fire.
> (Hays, 2009: 25)[2]

We see that Hays finds Descartes' philosophy liberating and emancipating, and a starting point for her own creative reflections.

Why Descartes was so popular among Early Modern women can be given several explanations. Descartes' language and construction of arguments were simple and accessible. He wrote in French and not in Latin, hence uneducated people, i.e. women could also read his works. The *method* he suggests was easily applicable on other areas. The mind/

body divide made the mind a sexless entity, the mind was disembodied. And, further, Descartes himself recognized learned women; he corresponded with the Swedish queen Kristina, Anna Maria van Schurmann and Elisabeth of Bohemia.

Perhaps most importantly; reason is given more power than the authority of tradition, which could be used to form rational arguments to fight women's traditional status as secondary.

The picture of Descartes as a proto-feminist thinker is reinforced by his discussion of generosity as a basis for morality in *Passions de l'âme* (*Passions of the Soul*). Moral conduct based on generosity necessarily leads to the idea that people ought to treat one another as equals.

The *cartésiennes* were numerous. Erica Harth, author of *Cartesian Women*, lists these names: Mme de Sévigné, her daughter Mme de Grignan, Mme de Coulanges, Mme de Vins, Mme d'Outresale, Mme d'Hommecour, Mme de Guedreville, Mme de Bonneveaux, Mme de Sablé, Mme de La Sablière, Mme Deshoulières, Mademoiselle de la Vigne, Mademoiselle Descartes (Descartes' niece, daughter of his brother Pierre), Mademoiselle Dupré and Mademoisele Wailly (Harth, 1992). Not all of these were salonnières themselves but frequented the most fashionable salons. Harth shows in her book how these women attempted to overcome gender barriers and participated in the shaping of rational discourse. Most of them are now forgotten.

The erasure of women's philosophical publications from the historical record is, by philosopher Eileen O'Neill, termed "disappearing ink" (O'Neill, 1997). In addition to the problems generated by the standard practice of anonymous authorship for women, O'Neill writes, the broader theoretical frameworks in which women's philosophical views had a place were relegated to the status of non-philosophy by the 19th century (O'Neill, 1997: 20). O'Neill points to a "purification" of philosophy taking place in the 18th century. While the woman question and theological questions alike were important parts of philosophy in the 17th century, by the 19th century philosophy had confined theology to its own domain and the woman question was no longer considered to be of philosophical interest (with perhaps the exception of Mary Wollstonecraft and John Stuart Mill, who will be discussed in the next chapter). These subjects fell out of the canon after the purification of the discipline. For Immanuel Kant and the philosophy in his footsteps, anything pre-critical reeks like an "over-perfumed" French salon.

The mind has no sex – François Poulain de la Barre

François Poulain de la Barre (1647–1723) brings the concept of equality to the thinking of Descartes. Simone de Beauvoir pays tribute to Poulain de la Barre (hereafter Poulain) by citing him on the title page of *The Second Sex* in 1949: "Everything that men have written about women should be viewed with suspicion because they are both judge and party". Unfortunately, this reference is omitted in the first English translation of Beauvoir's book, thus many English readers are probably unaware of Beauvoir's salutation to Poulain and early Cartesian feminism. In the history chapter of *The Second Sex* Beauvoir also calls Poulain "The period's most determined feminist" (Beauvoir, 2011: 126). While the idea of gender as a social construction is often portrayed as a recent feminist invention, or even a post-modern thought, this idea has a history dating back at least to Poulain and the European Enlightenment. In his pamphlet *On the Equality of the Two Sexes* (1673) Poulain sought to follow Descartes' methodological-epistemological ideas and distinguish between facts and custom, claiming that the alleged natural inequality between men and women was nothing but unfounded prejudice, i.e. socially constructed. Although he did not use the concepts "sex" and "gender", the essence of his argument corresponds to present discussions of the sex-gender divide. To distinguish between biological sex and social gender was possible on the basis of Cartesian philosophy. Poulain applied Cartesian principles to the so-called "woman question" and demonstrated by a rational deduction that it was prejudice and custom that governed the common and ordinary understanding of women. According to Poulain, women's "natural" subordination and inferiority was culturally produced. Old habits and lack of education makes us believe women are inferior to men, Poulain claims. People base their opinions on custom and not reason he writes. Poulain's argument has several affinities with the later Simone de Beauvoir's famous dictum "one is not born, but rather becomes, woman". Which is maybe why she paid tribute to him.

Poulain is for many people completely unknown, despite the fact that his writings constitute one of the most important stages in the development of feminist thought, and thus also a part of European intellectual history. So, who was François Poulain de la Barre? He was born in Paris in 1647 to a distinguished Catholic family. The family fortune saw to his education and his parents expected a career within the Church. After a degree in theology he grew deeply unsatisfied with scholastic philosophy and became a convinced Cartesian instead. After having served as a minister in the Champagne district he left the Catholic Church and converted to Protestantism, married and had two children. He died as a Calvinist in exile Geneva in 1723. But it was during his years as an unmarried Catholic vicar that he wrote and published three anonymous feminist essays: *On the Equality of the Two Sexes* (1673), *On the Education of Ladies* (1674) and *On the Excellence of Men* (1675).

52 Cartesian feminism

The subtitle of *On the Equality of the Two Sexes* carries an important message to its readers: "A Physical and Moral Discourse Which Shows the Importance of Getting Rid of One's Prejudices". The Cartesian methodological-epistemological ideal of overcoming prejudice is evident already in the Preface:

> We will offer proofs that a very deep-seated universal belief is the result of prejudice and error in order to convince readers to judge things for themselves and not let themselves be deceived by the opinions of others.
> Our choice fell on the question of the equality of the sexes, which is more prone to prejudice than any other subject.
> If we look at current attitudes towards men and women, we find that intellectual and professional distinctions are more likely to made than physical ones. The reason given for this discrimination in most writings is that women are incapable of playing any role in the sciences or in public life because they are not as intelligent as men. They deserve, therefore, their inferior status.
> We, however, propose to examine this idea by applying the rule of truth: accept nothing as true unless it is supported by clear and distinct ideas. Thus we find that the common prejudice is founded on mere popular hearsay, and that the two sexes *are* equal. Women have the same gifts of intelligence and energy as men.
> (Poulain, 2002: 50)

The text echoes Descartes' method and ambition of abolishing prejudice but it also echoes another thinker; Marie le Jars de Gournay and her idea of equality between men and women. Poulain is in many ways a blend of Descartes and Gournay. With Poulain, Descartes' method is applied to defend a view of equality shared by Gournay. According to historian Siep Stuurman, who has written a full volume on Poulain, Poulain is the first thinker to make equality a foundational concept of social philosophy. Poulain drew on natural-rights philosophy as well as strong egalitarian elements in Cartesiansim but transcended both according to Stuurman by making equality a critical socio-political concept. Thus, Poulain's essay represents the first formulation of a fully universalist concept of equality in European history. Stuurman suggests calling Poulain's theorization of equality *modern equality* (Stuurman, 2004). This again corresponds very well with the overall assumption of this book; to bring to light the history of *modern* feminism. According to Siep Stuurman, Poulain's texts were probably the most radically egalitarian texts published in Europe before the French Revolution.

Poulain begins his treatise by the primal antidote to Scholasticism; observation and experience. Observation and experience had revolutionized the natural sciences, empirical investigations had led to discoveries that completely changed the view of the world and the universe. To demonstrate how prejudices fill our minds and "that there are all kinds of things that men believe with no justification", Poulain begins his argument with an allusion to the Copernican system:

> Apart from a handful of scientists, everyone is convinced beyond doubt that it is the sun that moves around the earth. But anyone who has made a study of the revolution of days and years is equally convinced that it is the earth that moves around the sun.
> (Poulain, 2002: 52)

He then continues to claim that the discussion of the differences between the sexes up till now has been superficial and biased against women. But if a man were to reach objective and disinterested knowledge of women, he would realize that there are only a few natural indispositions that make women different from men. "On the other hand, he would see that the very appearances which, superficially considered, deceive people about women would convince him of the truth if he looked at them more closely" (ibid.). If we observed and studied women as closely as we study the stars, sun and the universe, we would reach a truth comparable to the discovery of Copernicus, Kepler and Galilei. The earth moves around the sun and men and women have equal mental capacities.[3]

The first part of Poulain's *Equality* essay is an investigation into what the prejudices of women are built upon. Here Poulain employs a kind of mixture of anthropological and historical method. He claims: "man's behavior towards women in all places and at all times is so uniform that it seems to be part of an organized movement" (ibid., 55). Such a universal phenomenon calls for a thorough investigation or what he calls "close analysis". The starting point for such an analysis is difficult because not only men but also women themselves seem to believe "that their minds are as different as their bodies". For Poulain it is simply the fact that men are physically stronger that has put them in a superior position. Being physically stronger led men to believe that they were superior in all respects. Quite reminiscent of Simone de Beauvoir's analysis in *The Second Sex*, Poulain begins his investigation in pre-historical times when men allegedly were hunters and lived their lives outdoors and women, due to childbirth, were obliged to remain indoors. This division of labour led to the exclusion of women in the first occupations, Poulain writes. He also points to the fact that there have existed learned women, but "they had no disciples or adherents, and all their learning died fruitlessly with them" (ibid., 59). There is nothing in women's *nature* that makes them inferior to men it is history and arbitrary circumstances, such as lack of education, that has passed upon women a subordinate position. Poulain draws a parallel with uneducated men and asks how many peasants might have become renowned scholars if they had been given the chance to study? Poulain also refers frequently to his own encounters and conversations with women. Based on his observation and experience, women are able to understand theology as well as medicine and law. Therefore it must be recognized that women are, in general, capable of scientific study. Having given a historical explanation of the difference or inequality between the sexes Poulain then moves on the crux of his text; the claim that the mind has no sex.

> It is easy to see that the difference between the two sexes is limited to the body, since that is the only part used in the reproduction of humankind. Since the mind merely gives its consent, and does so in exactly the same way in everyone, we can conclude that it has no sex.
> (Poulain, 2002: 82)

This argument would be practically impossible to advance without Cartesian dualism. Considered independently, Poulain continues, "the mind is found to be equal and of the same nature in all men, and capable of all kinds of thoughts" (ibid., 82). This is why we can claim that Descartes philosophy can be interpreted as liberating for women.

There are numerous facts to consider in order to understand Poulain and his opposition to gender conventions in 17th century France. One factor is France's absolute monarchy, and especially the absolutism of Louis XIV, which led to reductions of religious freedom as well as many limitations for women. The Edict of Nantes from 1785 actually prohibited freedom of religion and freedom of speech. Another factor is as already indicated, the philosophy of René Descartes. The absolute monarchy of the Sun King brought about a backlash for women. While women had played a significant role in the salon movement, they were excluded from the newly founded *Académie des sciences* (established by Louis XIV in 1699). The *Académie* was established to encourage and protect French scientific thought few years after the Roman Catholic Church had placed Descartes' works on the Index. There were accordingly conservative forces that wanted both to forbid Cartesian philosophy and also limit women's possibilities to study and take part in the development of society.

The rest of the chapter will present a few other examples of feminist reflection that followed in the wake of Descartes.

Mary Astell – a Cartesian and England's first feminist

Descartes was not only popular among French women. In England Mary Astell was influenced by Descartes and argued for the importance of education for women, as we saw in Chapter 2. Mary Astell is often referred to as England's first feminist (Patricia Springborg, 1996: xi), and her feminism is clearly indebted to Descartes. She proposed to establish a female academy where ladies could surround themselves with useful knowledge. Her book, *A Serious Proposal to the Ladies, For the Advancement of their True and Great Interest*, published in London in 1694, is yet another example of the importance of Cartesianism for the development of modern feminist thought.

Since God has given women as well as men intelligent souls, then why should they be forbidden to improve them, Astell asks rhetorically. Ladies who are already educated in the art of reading can do better than just reading novels and romances. They ought to adorn their minds with useful knowledge, such as that contained in the writing of Descartes, Astell suggests (Astell, 2002: 82).

Why should women waste their talents? A female academy for ladies would, according to Astell, help improve their charm and heighten their value: "Raise you above the Vulgar by something truely illustrious, than a sounding Title or a great Estate" (ibid., 51). Women should learn to pride themselves on something more excellent than the invention of a fashion. Astell sees education as the road to understanding and thus the lack of education as the source of women's ignorance: "Thus Ignorance and narrow Education lay the Foundation of Vice, and Imitation and Custom rear it up" (ibid., 67). As in the writings of Poulain we find the double explanation for women's inferior state in (a) their lack of education and (b) custom. After first giving reasons for her proposal and thereafter describing the suggested academy, Astell offers a method that is undoubtedly Cartesian:

> Disengage our selves from all our former Prejudices, from our Opinion of Names, Authorities, Customs and the like, not give credit to any thing any longer because we have once believ'd it, but because it carries clear and uncontested Evidence along with it.
> (ibid., 133)

According to Astell, prejudice is the grand hindrance in our search for truth, making us disposed to error. Using Cartesian arguments and methodology to promote her cause, Astell also suggests the reading of Descartes for her ladies' academy:

> And since the *French Tongue* is understood by most Ladies, methinks they may much better improve it by the study of Philosophy (as I hear the *French Ladies* do) *Des Cartes, Malebrance* and others, than by reading idle *Novel* and *Romances*.
>
> (ibid., 82–83)

Here Astell shows knowledge of French ladies reading Descartes. Her proposal for an academy for learned ladies was, however, never realised. For her contemporaries it resembled too much a Catholic nunnery. Not until Catherine the Great established the Smolny Institute in St. Petersburg in 1764 were women allowed to pursue higher education.

As Erica Harth claims in *Cartesian Women*, Descartes' philosophy was the first in France to attract a wide lay public of educated men and women (Harth, 1992). The appeal of Descartes' philosophy was his egalitarian epistemology, truth could be discovered by anyone, of either sex. This universalism about knowledge denies difference among knowers. For educated, upper-class women, his philosophy was like a "university without walls" (ibid., 3). Descartes' philosophy opened up a possibility of philosophical discussions with men that was previously denied to them.

Correspondence with Descartes – Elisabeth of Bohemia

Elisabeth of the Palatine, also known as Elisabeth of Bohemia (1618–1680), daughter of Kurfürst Friedrich V. von der Pfalz, the king of Bohemia, is known for her philosophical correspondence with Descartes. Their correspondence lasted until Descartes' death in 1650. That their friendship was an affectionate one is clear from how Descartes signed his letters: "Le très humble et très obeisant serviteur" (Your very affectionate friend at your service).

Elisabeth is best known for challenging Descartes' dualism. Between 1643 and 1649 Descartes and Princess Elisabeth of Bohemia exchanged 58 letters, 32 of which were written by Descartes and 26 by Elisabeth. This correspondence reveals Elisabeth as one of the first to pose the mind-body problem in questioning how mind and body causally interact with another, i.e. how two distinct substances can causally interact. Having read Descartes' *Meditations* Elisabeth wrote to him and asked: "So I ask you please to tell me how the soul of a human being (it being only a thinking substance) can determine the bodily spirits, in order to bring about voluntary actions" (Elisabeth of Bohemia, 2007: 62). From a feminist point of view, Elisabeth's questioning is even more fascinating given that she argues from the point of view of pregnancy:

> For even if we were to suppose them inseparable (which is however difficult to prove in *the mother's womb* and in great fainting spells) as are the attributes of God, we could, in considering them apart, acquire a more perfect idea of them.
>
> (ibid., my italics)

Three weeks later Descartes replied in a letter to Elisabeth:

> For there are two things about the human soul on which all the knowledge we can have of its nature depends: one of which is that it thinks, and the other is that, being united to the body, it can act on and be acted upon by it.
>
> (ibid., 64–65)

But Elisabeth was not satisfied with his reply and asks again in her next letter how the soul, if completely distinguished from the body the way Descartes describes it, is still governed by and acts upon the body. If the mind and body are two separate entities, then how do they interact with each other? Descartes never provided a satisfying answer to this question. Mind-body dualism continued to be a problem for Elisabeth and when writing to Descartes about her personal problems – melancholy and physical ailments – Descartes suggested a psychosomatic cure: thinking positive thoughts.

Discussions have been raised regarding whether Elisabeth is to be regarded as a philosopher in her own right, or whether she is simply a Cartesian muse. From a feminist point of view, uncovering the ideas of women that have previously been overlooked can change the picture of the history of philosophy as an exclusively male enterprise. Uncovering the works of minor figures helps to fill in the gaps in the history of philosophy and provide a richer picture.

A Nordic Cartesian feminist – Ludvig Holberg

Ludvig Holberg (1684–1754) was the most successful author of his age in Scandinavia. His works were translated into German, French and English. He has been termed the most European of Scandinavian writers before

Henrik Ibsen.[4] He is sometimes referred to as the "father" of Norwegian and Danish literature, or the "Moliére of the North".[5] Ludvig Holberg was a true Enlightenment thinker, radical and critical of all conventions including the gender hierarchy. That Holberg not only defended women but also was a radical feminist, and wrote a history of famous women, seems to be relatively unknown, even among Nordic feminists and gender researchers. His take on the question of women places him within a Cartesian equality discourse with thinkers like Poulain.

It is challenging to get hold of Holberg's views on the woman question; he never wrote one text particularly dedicated to the issue, his views on the matter are scattered all over his writings. In 1745, however, he published *Several Heriones' and Noteworthy Ladies' Compared Histories*, which is a collection of great women through history in the tradition of Bocaccio.[6] The women in this volume are set out as examples of what women are able to do given the chance. Holberg's listing of women has much in common with Marie de Gournay's listing of great women. Paradoxically, perhaps, it is in Holberg's *Several Great Heroes' and Famous Men's Compared Histories,* wherein he also includes portraits of two great women, that is most explicit about his views on women. It cannot be denied that one sex is weaker than the other, he writes, but if we put too much into this women might conclude that since men are physically stronger they must do all the manual labouring, while women can take care of the more subtle tasks. One might even get the idea that women are better suited to drawing and planning a building while men are better suited to carrying bricks, carpentry and tasks where physical strength is needed. Holberg claims that it is habit and upbringing that makes us believe that women are naturally inferior to men. If women were given the same upbringing as men, they would have been just as clever.

The satirical imaginary voyage, *The journey of Niels Klim to the World Underground*, is where we find Holberg's most radical feminist ideas. His ideas were so radical and provocative that the novel had to be published anonymously. The first English version appeared in 1742, only a year after the original publication of the work. The English translation was so successful that it was reprinted three times within the next years. One of the countries Niels Klim visits is Potu (Utop[ia] spelled backwards), and here women govern and decide. The method of presenting radical ideas about women through an imagined ideal state is something we recognize from Plato's *Republic* and Christine de Pizan's *City of Ladies.*

Among Holberg scholars it is generally accepted that he was acquainted with the philosophy of Descartes, although we do not know for certain exactly what he had read (Jensen, 1984: 70). Holberg also seems to have adopted Poulain's thesis that the mind has no sex. The question of intertextuality is challenging in connection with authors who do not necessarily operate with rich references. A later feminist writer who might have been inspired by Holberg again is Condorcet, who will be discussed in the next chapter. Condorcet's arguments and use of irony resembles conspicuously those of Holberg, and we know that Holberg was widely read in France.

A 20th century feminist Cartesian – Simone de Beauvoir

Sitting at Café Les Deux Magots, reading, writing or relaxing with a drink looking across the square to the St. Germain des Prés church where Descartes lies buried, Beauvoir must have reflected from time to time on this "father of modern philosophy". In the following I will suggest that there is a clear affinity between Simone de Beauvoir and René Descartes in one important aspect; the effort and will to overcome prejudice, or in the words of Beauvoir, myths. This is also an ambition Beauvoir shares with Poulain and another reason for her to salute him in *The Second Sex*.

Nancy Bauer has previously pointed to affinities between Descartes and Beauvoir, drawing attention especially to the role of doubt: "Descartes will doubt all his opinions; Beauvoir whether women exist" (Bauer, 2001: 68). They both build their philosophy on a scepticist foundation. Just as Descartes's cogito rests on an "I" that doesn't doubt his existence, Beauvoir's theses rests on an "I" that doesn't doubt being a woman, but rather certifies that "I am a woman".

There is yet another way in which Beauvoir's philosophy can be seen as a continuation or development of the philosophical tradition of Descartes and Poulain and that is by their efforts to abolish and overcoming prejudices. According to Beauvoir, the project in *The Second Sex* is to abolish "the myth of the eternal feminine". In fact, the whole of Modernity can be described as an overall attempt to replace myth with facts and truth. Enlightenment is often described as the overcoming of myth through critique.

The myth of the eternal feminine has, according to Beauvoir, no origin in nature, but in human history. This is also what she expresses by devoting five chapters to history in part called "facts and myths" in *The Second Sex*.

This chapter has tried to show how inspiring and important Descartes was for 17th and 18th century feminism. Cartesianism provided a basis for a radical egalitarianism of women's and men's minds, or modes of reasoning. Descartes' dualism, which has received harsh criticism by 20th century feminists, was experienced as liberating and promising by earlier generations of women.

Notes

1 See e.g. Nicholas Jolley: "The reception of Descartes' philosophy" in John Cottingham (ed.) *The Cambridge Companion to Descartes*. Cambridge University Press, Cambridge, 1992.
2 Thanks to colleague Tone Brekke for bringing my attention to Mary Hays.
3 The allusion to the Copernican revolution as a metaphor for male prejudices against women has later also been employed by Luce Irigaray in her essay "Any Theory of the 'Subject' Has Always Been Appropriated by the 'Masculine'" where she claims: "The Copernican revolution has yet to have its final effects in the male imaginary" (Irigaray: [1974] 1985, 133).
4 P.M. Mitchell explains the lack of awareness of Holberg's name in the English-speaking world to be sought in part in the marked parallelism between his ideas and those of his English contemporaries (Mitchell, 1991).
5 He is claimed by both Norway and Denmark, which were united at the time. Holberg was born in Bergen in Norway but settled (after many years of travelling in Europe) in Copenhagen, which was then the capital of the two united countries.
6 The listing of famous women from history is a "tradition" going back to Italian Renaissance writer Giovanni Bocaccio's *Famous Women* (*De mulieribus claris*) of 1362. Bocaccio's work is the first collection of biographies in Western literature devoted exclusively to women. Bocaccio's *Famous Women* inspired a wave of catalogues of great women. See Chapter 2.

4 Citizenship, education and the vote

Enlightenment – the age of reason

> *Habit can so familiarize men with violations of their natural rights that those who have lost them neither think of protesting nor believe they are unjustly treated.*

These words were written by the French Marquis de Condorcet in his essay *On Giving Women the Right to Citizenship* in 1790. Condorcet argued in favour of gender equality and the civil and political rights of women. The quote makes a suitable transition from last chapter's focus on Cartesianism and the many feminist efforts to overcome prejudice and custom to this chapter's focus on citizenship and the right to vote. The topic of citizenship will be explored mainly through three 18th and 19th century feminist thinkers who contributed in different ways to developing and sharpening the arguments that finally won women political rights in the 20th century. Marquis de Condorcet, Mary Wollstonecraft and John Stuart Mill were all, as we shall see, deeply connected to the philosophical thinking of their day. The French Revolution, Enlightenment philosophy, British empiricism and the development of utilitarianism, all were important for the development of the modern idea of gender equality. Like the previous chapters, this chapter aims to show the close connection between philosophical innovations and feminism.

Discussions of gender and citizenship have a long history and go back to Antiquity, e.g. Plato's *Republic* and Sophocle's tragedy *Antigone*. Antigone is one of Western culture's first literary heroines, and Plato famously suggested including women in the organization of the ideal state of *The Republic*. Citizenship signifies membership in a political community, Greek city-state or polis, a medieval city or the modern nation-state. It denotes an exclusive status, setting boundaries between who's in or out. Citizenship defines the status of a person as a

62 Citizenship, education and the vote

legal member of a sovereign state, nation, polis or city. As a citizen one has rights, such as the right to vote, but must also follow the laws (and customs) of the state or city of which one is a citizen.[1]

The idea that everyone should have a say, or a right to vote, followed a new focus on the individual in European thought. Protestant theology asserted that man's relationship to God was an individual one, and that everyone, male or female, must stand individually before God. Claims to rights rest in many ways on one's status as an individual. In modern philosophy the individual, or subject, is increasingly more often the focal point. For Descartes, it was the cogito, the thinking that constituted the subject and laid the foundation of all knowledge. Kant demonstrates with his "Copernican Turn" that empirical knowledge relies on the innate subjective structure of how we come to know. For the thinkers of the Enlightenment, it is the right to vote, or citizenship, that literally constitutes the subject – the subject understood as male, that is.

The French Revolution established the principle of equal national citizenship. From the view of feminism, the topic of citizenship has since the French Revolution been a question of struggle for women's right to vote and become full members of society. The discussions of women's full political participation that began with the French Revolution had by the end of the 19th century grown into a pan-European/Western discussion of women's suffrage.

French and European philosophy in and around the time of the French Revolution was deeply political. Radical ideas were exchanged between European countries, particularly between France and England. John Locke's ideas inspired French thinkers, and the French Enlightenment inspired British philosophy. New ideas and thoughts also travelled the continent and overseas to America. The American Revolution, or Declaration of Independence from 1783, greatly inspired the later French Revolution of 1789. Ideas of human rights, educational and institutional reforms and hopes for a rational and democratic polity were the backbone of the philosophical thinking of the day. This epoch represents a decisive shift in the history of ideas in modern times. The Enlightenment has been described as "a revolution of the mind", crediting the Enlightenment thinkers with a decisive turning-point in history (Israel, 2010). One primary aim of the Enlightenment philosophers was to abolish privilege and rank, render society more "enlightened", and thereby transform the political and social framework of modern life. They grounded the egalitarian and democratic core values and ideals of the modern world, the ideas that still underlie Western societies. It must, however, also be mentioned that the development of Enlightenment reason also provided a rationale for slavery, based on a hierarchy of races, although slavery was strongly opposed by those who gave voice to the rights of women.

The Enlightenment, or "the Age of Reason", was dedicated to human progress and the advancement of the natural sciences. The idea of relying on reason alone arrives in the wake of scientific revolutions. The human mind had proved its ability to explain the external world independent of religion and faith. This carried forward an 18th century politics and philosophy that sought to undermine tradition and re-educate people. Faith in reason and education are two core elements within Enlightenment thinking, and the backdrop for German philosopher Immanuel Kant's interpretation of Enlightenment in 1784 as "Sapere aude!" meaning "dare to know". People should be inspired to have the courage to use their own mind. They should dare to use their own understanding without guidance.

Before moving on to Condorcet and the French Revolution, a few words on Jean Jacques Rousseau (1712–1778) are imperative. The writings of Rousseau, in addition to those of John Locke (1632–1704), sparked in many ways both the American and the French Revolution. Rousseau brought forth the idea of natural human rights: "Man is born free, and everywhere he is in chains", he famously wrote in 1762 (Rousseau, 1973: 181). Rousseau was one of the most influential thinkers during the Enlightenment in 18th century Europe (although it can be argued that Rousseau was anti-Enlightenment with his emphasis on nature and sensibility). The development towards democracy and human rights owes in many ways gratitude to Rousseau, but regarding the question of women there was conspicuously little to find in Rousseau, as we shall see. In the essay *Discourse on Inequality* (1755) Rousseau sets out to trace the origin and development of inequality and endeavour to show that in the state of nature inequality is almost non-existent. Inequality exists because some people enjoy privileges at the expense of others. Discussing inequality in this work, Rousseau never drew any conclusions regarding the inequality between the sexes, but argues as follows:

> The human species has, I think, two sorts of inequality: the one I call natural or physical because it is established by nature, and consists of difference in age, health, physical strength, and traits of the mind or soul; the other kind we can call moral or political inequality, for it depends on a sort of convention and is established, or at least sanctioned, by the consent of men. This inequality consists of the various privileges that some persons enjoy at the expense of others.
>
> (ibid., 23)

Although Rousseau here does not speak about sex, it is clear if we analyze this against the background of his later writings that he regards sex as a difference belonging to the first category, i.e. natural/physical. All sex differences are only natural.

In his writings, Rousseau does not just forget women nor quietly silence them, but actively places them outside of the political sphere. Rousseau develops theories on how we can have a more democratically based politics and achieve equality, but he completely leaves women out. Enlightenment feminists inspired by his work were disappointed by his ideas on women and the upbringing of girls. In Rousseau's book on education, *Émile* (1762), he aims to show how a child can be brought up free from aggression and willing to cooperate with others. The first four chapters of the book are dedicated to the boy Émile and his upbringing, while the last chapter addresses Émile's female companion, Sophie, and the upbringing of girls. Men and women are different by nature, Rousseau thinks, hence this difference must be further cultivated. Women are made to please and be governed by men, thus men and women must be given very different upbringing and education. Today *Émile* more or less reads like instructions for how to manipulate women into subordination. In Rousseau's view, women exist primarily for the service of men. As we shall see, Mary Wollstonecraft strongly opposes Rousseau, as does the Marquis de Condorcet.

Philosopher of human rights and female citizenship – Condorcet

Marie Jean Antoine Nicolas de Caritat, Marquis de Condorcet (1743–1794), French philosopher, mathematician and political scientist, represents one of the earliest proposals of giving women the right to citizenship and vote. Condorcet lived, worked and wrote in the Enlightenment era, the intellectual and social movement that culminated in the French Revolution. The French wanted to replace the *ancien régime* with a new government based on Enlightenment ideas of liberty and equality. All kinds of hierarchies – from monarchy, aristocracy and woman's subordination to man – were challenged. Ideas of equality, tolerance, democracy and individual freedom challenged the monarchy, aristocracy, authority and tradition. The relationship between the sexes had also begun to change. The salon movement encouraged an interaction between the sexes that became popular, even fashionable. The salons were run by intellectual women and became a platform and opportunity for women to exchange arguments and ideas. Women could not enter academies and universities, but the salons offered an opportunity to discuss matters such as politics, philosophy and science. The early phase of the French Revolution saw numerous women's clubs being established. And a general growing interest in women took place. Male writers of the Enlightenment focused intensively on "women" and "women's nature". Various interpretations and views were discussed by figures like Montesquieu, Voltaire, Diderot, Rousseau, Condorcet and Kant, to mention but a few. The time seemed ripe to address the question of women's rights and participation in the public. Rousseau had eliminated women from public life by confining them to private and domestic roles. These are some of the events that make up the background and frame for Condorcet.

Condorcet is often referred to as the last of *philosophes*. The *philosophes* being French Enlightenment thinkers, not philosophers in the strict sense of the word, but intellectuals who expressed support for social, economic and political reforms, and convinced believers of the supremacy and efficacy of human reason. Among the *philosophes* were also prominent figures like Montesqieu, Voltaire, Rousseau and Diderot. One of their famous achievements was the *Encyclopédie*, an ambitious project intended to gather and organize all of the world's essential knowledge, and thus a democratization of knowledge. Condorcet was an advocate of educational reform and women's rights and was the most outspoken French feminist since Poulain de la Barre. He was one of few Enlightenment ideologists to witness the French Revolution and participate as an elected politician at the centre of the events during France's transition from monarchy to republic.

Condorcet came from a family of minor aristocracy. He studied mathematics at the university of Paris, specializing in probability calculus. Under the patronage of d'Alambert, Condorcet was admitted to the Academy of Science in 1769. Influenced by both Voltaire and Turgot, he was drawn into politics and became a member of the National Assembly. He married Sophie de Grouchy (1764–1822), who was 20 years younger, and with whom he is reported to have had a loving marriage and intellectual partnership. Sophie collaborated on Condorcet's writings, as well as translating the works of Adam Smith and Thomas Paine, and writing her own books. The Condorcets ran their own salon in Paris, which hosted many foreign and prominent visitors e.g. the later American president Thomas Jefferson, the philosopher Thomas Paine, the playwright and pamphleteer Olympe de Gouges and writer and hostess Madame de Staël. Their salon was an important venue for revolutionary groups during the early years of the Revolution.

Condorcet voted against the execution of King Louis XVI, as he opposed the death penalty. After having criticized the Jacobin Robespierre, Condorcet was charged with conspiracy in 1793 and called for arrest. He fled and spent the remaining six months of his life hiding.[2] By this time, all the leading Girondins, i.e. Condorcet's friends, had been guillotined. He was eventually captured and was found dead in his cell in March 1794.

Condorcet, like Descartes and Poulain before him, was disappointed with his Jesuit education and went from supporting constitutional monarchy to defending a democratic republic based on universal suffrage. He not only supported property-based franchise but also supported the equality of women and black slaves. Having changed his interests over the years from mathematics to human rights, he was a committed and enthusiastic defender of human rights. He drafted numerous bills for the National Assembly as well as a constitution for France. It was in his 1787 *Letters from a Freeman of New Haven to a Citizen of Virginia on the Futility of Dividing the Legislative Power among Several Bodies* that he first formulated a proposal for constitutional rights for women. But it is the short text *On Giving Women the Right of Citizenship* from 1790 that secures Condorcet a place in the genealogy of feminist thinking. This is indeed the very first proposition ever of giving women rights to vote!

Chapter 2 suggested that the development of the concept of equality was based on mathematical advancements and Enlightenment thoughts and ideals that coalesced in the 17th century. Condorcet brings the intertwinement of mathematics and social development a step further by his "social mathematics". Condorcet suggested that the application of calculus as an instrument for prediction could facilitate the development of a science of political management (Williams, 2004: 104). Once again, as in the case of Descartes, we see how training in logic and mathematics offered a background against which to unfold democratic ideas.

Condorcet was exceptional, even for an Enlightenment thinker. He extended the new ideas of liberty and equality to women and argued in favour of giving women rights to citizenship, thereby giving men and women equal rights. He argued that custom made people – including philosophers and legislators – blind to the fact that one half of the human race had lost or been deprived of their natural rights.

> The rights of men stem exclusively from the fact that they are sentient beings, capable of acquiring moral ideas and of reasoning upon them. Since women have the same qualities, they necessarily also have the same rights, or else they all have the same ones; and anyone who votes against the rights of another, whatever his religion, colour or sex, automatically forfeits his own.
> (Condorcet, 2012: 156)

Condorcet makes his point by use of sharp arguments and irony. For example, he points out that while it is said that no woman has made any important discovery in science, or has given any proof of genius in arts, literature, etc., no one has ever suggested that citizenship should be accorded only to men of genius! If knowledge and reason are set as qualifications for obtaining citizenship, then those men who are devoted to constant labour and can neither acquire knowledge nor exercise their reason must also be deprived of their rights.

When women have been excluded from public affairs, then they also lack the experience that comes from exercising these rights. But in a great number of countries, Condorcet continues, women have been judged incapable of all public functions, and yet worthy of royalty. Think only of Elizabeth of England, Maria Theresia and the two Catherines of Russia – have they not shown that neither in courage nor in strength of mind are women wanting? This shows that when given the chance women can perform just as well as men. In the same manner as Marie de Gournay and Ludvig Holberg before him, Condorcet lists several learned ladies as examples of women's capacities, one of which is Marie de Gournay.

A recurrent argument in favour of expanding possibilities and rights for women has been to point to learned ladies of the past as examples of what women can accomplish when given the chance. Writing catalogues of learned ladies goes back, as we have seen, to the Italian Renaissance writer Giovanni Bocaccio's *De muleribus Claris* (*On famous women*) from 1362. Bocaccio's anthology consists of 106 examples of famous women from Antiquity to the Middle Ages. While Bocaccio praised learned women as exceptions to their sex, later listings of famous women serve as calls for education for all girls, perhaps especially in the works of Marie de Gournay, Mary Astell and Condorcet. These lists of learned women serve as a kind of campaign stating that "Women can!" – a message that was equally directed towards men as well as women.

In Condorcet's view it is not nature, but lack of education and experience that produces a difference between the two sexes. This argument places him in the footsteps of the earlier Poulain and anticipates the writings of Mary Wollstonecraft. Condorcet argues for complete equality between men and women and thus contributes to France's transition into Modernity (Williams, 2004). Through Condorcet's Enlightenment narrative of reason, equality, tolerance and humanity, subjects are turned into citizens. The subject becomes a citizen in the sense of being a participating agent in the exercise of state politics. Liberty for men only was for Condorcet a partial liberty; full liberty for all or universal liberty would not be completed until women won the same right. Condorcet was a bold and courageous writer, quite unafraid to say what he thought. His ideas were far from mainstream opinion; he even defended homosexuality, claiming that sodomy ought not to be regarded as a crime because it did not violate the rights of any other man (Condorcet, 1994: 56). This indicates the radicalness of his liberalism.

Condorcet was ahead of his time. His idea of giving women a political voice was not realized in France until women won the vote in 1945, 155 years after Condorcet's proposition. Neither Condorcet's writings nor the Revolution resulted in any prompt change for women. As the later Simone de Beauvoir remarked in *The Second Sex*: "The Revolution might have been expected to change the fate of woman. It did nothing of the kind" (Beauvoir, 2011: 128). Condorcet's essay was forgotten until British suffragettes rediscovered the text in 1894 and translated it into English. But Condorcet nevertheless deserves a place in the historical account of the development of feminist thought.

As we all know, the quest for equality in France resulted in a revolution, and the development of the rights of man. French human rights declared that all are born equal, all have the right to liberty, property and protection against oppression, but they neither addressed nor mentioned women. The playwright Olympe de Gouges and Condorcet were both members of "Society of the friends of truth", a revolutionary society that fought for equal rights also for women. They both also engaged themselves in the battle against slavery in America. Olympe de Gouges (1748–1793) accordingly formulated her own "rights of woman" as she interpreted the Revolution's rights of man or "droits de l'homme" as literally rights for men only. De Gouges was excited about the Revolution, but disappointed that it ignored women. Her *Declaration of women's rights* begins by determining: "Woman is born free..." mirroring the *Declaration of Rights of Man*, "Man is born free..."

After the murder of the revolutionary leader Marat, all women's clubs in France were banned. A young woman, Charlotte Corday, assassinated in 1793 the radical Jacobin Jean-Paul Marat while he was taking a bath, immortalized by Jacques-Louis David's painting *The Death of Marat* from the same year. Corday hoped that assassinating Marat would put an end the violence and terror in France. People were shocked and astonished by what a woman was able to do, but her actions did little to make way for women's case. The national convent answered by banning all women's clubs and sent Corday along with Olympe de Gouges to the guillotine (Offen, 1994: 56).

A philosopher and a woman – Mary Wollstonecraft

In her famous essay "A Room of One's Own", Virginia Woolf writes:

> Towards the end of the eighteenth century a change came about which, if I were rewriting history, I should describe more fully and think of greater importance than the Crusades or the War of the Roses. The middle-class women began to write.
>
> (Woolf, 2008: 84)

Mary Wollstonecraft (1759–1797) is exemplary of those history-making women. In her mind women deserved to be full citizens and she thus advocated women's political inclusion. This section discusses Wollstonecraft in light of the philosophical background of her time: British empiricism.

Wollstonecraft was born in London as the second of seven children. Her father had squandered his inheritance and was a tyrannical man who drank heavily; Mary often had to protect her mother from his violent outburst. Her formal schooling was limited. Driven by the family's financial problems, she resolved to make her own way. Having twice tried to establish schools for girls and also tried working as a governess, she took on a life course supporting herself as a writer. Wollstonecraft became a member of the radical circle around the *Analytical Review* and its author Joseph Johnson. She was involved in the publication as reviewer and editorial assistant. In this way she became conversant with contemporary Enlightenment debates and translated books from French and German into English. Even though she had no formal education, Wollstonecraft was an intellectual woman well situated in the midst of contemporary philosophy and political debates. Through Johnson she met several radicals, such as the poet William Blake, the Swiss painter Henry Fuselli, the philosophers William Godwin and the revolutionary Thomas Paine. In 1792 Wollstonecraft moved to Paris to observe and document the Revolution. She wanted to see freedom being born but was horrified by the terror. She stayed in France for three years writing and meeting with the members of the Revolution; she apparently also seems to have met with Condorcet. While in Paris she met the American businessman Gilbert Imlay and had a child with him. The affair did not last, and Wollstonecraft returned to London in 1795 alone with her daughter Fanny. While recovering from the affair with Imlay she took her daughter on a Scandinavian expedition, producing the work *Letters Written During a Short Residence in Sweden, Norway and Denmark*. Shortly after her return from Scandinavia she met with William Godwin, whom she had met previously. In 1797 they married and a few months later Mary gave birth to her baby who grew up to be Mary Shelley, the author of *Frankenstein*. Ten days after the birth, at the age of thirty-eight, Mary Wollstonecraft died painfully of puerperal fever. Wollstonecraft is usually discussed in the context of liberalism, which is natural given her focus on freedom and personal autonomy. While this is entirely adequate, she also has a place within the context of British empiricism. The empiricists believed that all knowledge must be based on observation and experience: all hypothesis must be tested against observations. The motivation for this empiricist epistemology is to overcome prejudices. Wollstonecraft represents a consolidation between French Enlightenment and British Empiricism. Before moving on to her engaging work, it is necessary to have a short look at some of the highlights of British empiricism, which, together with French Enlightenment, constitutes the background of her thinking.

John Locke had argued in the late 17th century that the mind is a blank sheet or tabula rasa on which experiences leave their marks. He thus denied the Cartesian claim that the mind possesses innate ideas and held that anything knowable ultimately rests on sensory experience. David Hume continues the project of Locke by examining how knowledge is possible and the principles that regulate our understanding. Newton being his role model, Hume concludes that the only solid foundation we can give to science must be laid on experience and observation. Experience and observation are the two core concepts of empiricism. Already in the first paragraph of the Introduction of Mary Wollstonecraft's *Vindication of the Rights of Woman* we come across the verb "observe". Specifically, she has observed the conduct of parents and management of schools and concludes that the lack of education is the source of women's misery. She contrasts her own thoughts against what she calls "hasty conclusions". What has been written so far on women has primarily been written by men, and besides it is written with the goal to make women alluring mistresses rather than affectionate wives and rational mothers. Men have only their own interests at heart when they write about women. Wollstonecraft, by contrast, rests her arguments on experience and observation.

British empiricism does not only provide Wollstonecraft with concepts, theories and a method. The core content of empiricism – that all knowledge is based on sensory experience – offers an important strategy for defending feminism. Empiricism implies that the senses do not differ in man, nor between men and women. The point is to overcome prejudice and lay the foundation of a universal knowledge and science. The point of linking Wollstonecraft to the empiricist tradition is among other things to show that she was no outsider nor secluded thinker, but rather that her writings were part of an ongoing debate, and that she used concepts and arguments of the theories and philosophies of her time. Empiricism gives her the method, and the Enlightenment inspires the content and ideas of her thinking. This places her well within the canon of Western philosophical thinking.

Mary Wollstonecraft refers notably to herself in her work as a woman and a philosopher. "I am a woman" (1995: 75) and "As a philosopher" (ibid., 104). Being a woman and a philosopher is the foundation upon which she builds her observations and arguments. By presenting herself this way she establishes a persona as an educated woman whose opinions matter. Wollstonecraft begins her now feminist classic *A Vindication of the Rights of Woman* (1792) by demanding that women are treated as rational creatures and writes that her aim is to persuade her readers by the force of rational arguments. Wollstonecraft's contemporaries believed women were intellectually inferior to men. Wollstonecraft argues and insists that women are born equal to men and that the inequalities between the sexes can be erased by giving women access to education.

John Locke exercised great influence on the Enlightenment as well as on Mary Wollstonecraft. His three most famous works influenced Wollstonecraft: *Two Treatises of Government* (1690), *Essay Concerning Human Understanding* (1690), and *Some Thoughts on Education* (1693). John Locke's works provide Wollstonecraft with an understanding of natural rights, social contract, empiricist epistemology, and the importance of educating children from an early age.

The title of her major feminist work, *A Vindication of the Rights of Woman*, leads one to expect that the book will be about rights and equal rights between men and women. However, the book is mainly about female upbringing and education. She is more concerned with the reform of education than with establishing political and civil rights. The focus on education also places her well within the Enlightenment project. *Vindication* was dedicated to (and written as a response to) Talleyrand,[3] who in the fall of 1791 had presented a plan for public education to the French Assembly, but only for males. This shows how Wollstonecraft conversed with persons and ideas of her time. Her text is full of passages of dialogue and openings towards other thinkers and writers. Her primary proponent throughout the text is however Rousseau.

> "Educate women like men", says Rousseau, "and the more they resemble our sex the less power will they have over us." This is the very point I am at. I do not wish them to have power over men; but over themselves.
>
> (ibid., 138)

That Rousseau is one of the chief targets of Wollstonecraft's discussion is clear. She refers to him several times, e.g. when claiming that women require virtues "by the *same* means as men, instead of being educated like a fanciful *half* being – one of Rousseau's wild chimeras" (ibid., 110). She takes her own observations as point of departure to argue against Rousseau: "I have probably had an opportunity of observing more girls in their infancy than J.J. Rousseau" (ibid.). In the last section on Condorcet we saw how Rousseau wrote that boys and girls must be brought up radically different. Wollstonecraft argues against Rousseau, writing that it cannot be demonstrated that woman is essentially inferior to man, because she has always been subjugated. Wollstonecraft's claim is that we cannot really know what a woman de facto or in reality is, because until now she has only been the result of male fantasies. This has much in common with the thinking of the later John Stuart Mill and 20th century philosopher Luce Irigaray, as we shall see later.

According to Wollstonecraft, women have been lured into believing that being pretty and pleasing men is their foremost important responsibility. Both women and men must take responsibility for this false belief, and for changing it. Wollstonecraft states that many women are both silly and superficial, but this is not because of an innate deficiency, but because of lack of education, and here she joins the arguments of the earlier Mary Astell. Women have not been allowed to develop their faculties in the same way that men have. Women have been raised to a false and excessive sensibility. Wollstonecraft urges women to wake up and extend their interests to politics and other important matters. Society treats women as lesser beings, gives them poor education and training, thereafter accusing them of having little knowledge of things, she writes; it is thus time for a revolution in female manners. In a true Enlightenment spirit, Wollstonecraft argues that girls ought to be given training and education from an early age, as we saw in Chapter 2.

Not only have women not been given education, but Wollstonecraft compares women's condition to slavery. This might sound extreme, but in Wollstonecraft's days women had no legal rights. Legally speaking they could be separated from their children, locked up, beaten up, and raped by their husbands. Women lived on the mercy of their husbands and fathers. It was up to husband and father to treat them well. She goes as far as to compare marriage to prostitution. Where John Locke argued against the tyranny of kings over men, Wollstonecraft argues against the tyranny of men over women.

Wollstonecraft wanted women to aspire to full citizenship, and to be worthy of it. To this end they had to be given education and opportunity to develop their rational capacities. Regrettably Wollstonecraft's radical ideas and writings fell into oblivion until she was rediscovered by 20th century feminists. John Stuart Mill never refers to Mary Wollstonecraft, even though his ideas are very much related to hers. Her husband and widower William Godwin wrote a memoir of her after her death. Its frankness and emotional honesty provoked outrage and scandal and contributed to the oblivion of Wollstonecraft. Until the 20th century she was practically forgotten and ignored, and rather used as an example or warning of what could happen to a woman who let herself be ruled by passion (she had had a child out of wedlock).

Mary Wollstonecraft extends the project of liberalism and empiricism to the area of women, marriage, the relation between the sexes and the education of girls. She contributes to a universalizing of Enlightenment ideals. Where Condorcet placed the source of women's subordination to habit, in the company of Poulain, Wollstonecraft ascribes it to prejudices and lack of education.

A Victorian liberal – John Stuart Mill

With John Stuart Mill, the history or genealogy of feminism enters the 19th century and the Victorian era. It was after the publication of Mill's *The Subjection of Women* in 1869 that the campaign for women's right to vote saw a breakthrough all over the Western world. The book is today a classic in the history of philosophy and feminism alike, but it provoked fierce debates when it was first published. Confirmation of its challenge is proved by the fact that it was Sigmund Freud who translated the book into German.

Mill has two main targets in the book: the denial of political rights for women, and the inequality within marriage. Like Wollstonecraft, Mill was strongly opposed to the situation and disabilities of married women. He does not only argue for equal rights and opportunities for women but insists that the lack of such is crucial for the improvement of humanity: "the legal subordination of one sex to the other – is wrong in itself, and now one of the chief hindrances to human improvement" (Mill, 1988: 1). According to Mill, the system that rests on custom and the law of the strongest is a hindrance for the further development of society. We no longer believe that humans are born to their place in life, but that they are free to employ their faculties. Why is this not the case for women? In the Victorian era, the subordination of women was explained by women's nature, as it had been in previous centuries. Nature, Mill argues, is artificial, and we cannot know the nature of the two sexes, as they have only been seen in their present relation to one another. Mill compares the situation of married women to that of slavery. Although there are many similarities between Mill and Wollstonecraft, he surprisingly never refers to her. That we cannot know the true nature of women, because they have always been subordinated to men, and that marriage is comparable to slavery are both ideas we find in the writings of Wollstonecraft. One can speculate whether Godwin's honest portrait of Wollstonecraft and the scandal it gave rise to kept Mill from mentioning her. In any case, several of Mill's arguments are very similar to Wollstonecraft's. An obvious difference between the two is that while Wollstonecraft's text is overloaded, sometimes hard to follow and much too long, Mill's is short and to the point.

In many ways Mill stands as an antidote to Rousseau: "What is now called the nature of women is an eminently artificial thing – the result of forced repression in some directions, unnatural stimulations in others" (ibid., 22). Rousseau as we remember argued that women were naturally different to men and therefore ought to be educated very differently with the intention of becoming pleasing to men. For Mill, the subordination of women is only due to the interest of men and "because the generality of the male sex cannot tolerate the idea of living with an equal" (ibid., 53).

John Stuart Mill has been called Britain's major philosopher of the 19th century, continuing the British empiricist and liberalist traditions. As the oldest son of the philosopher James Mill, he was given a thorough education in classics, logic, political economy, jurisprudence and psychology. He grew up surrounded by a circle of political radicals, which included his father's friend Jeremy Bentham. Mill continued in the utilitarian footsteps of his father and Bentham, the utilitarian idea being roughly that the morally right action is that which produces the greatest amount of happiness for the greatest number of people. With his feminist writings, Mill thus expands the scope of utilitarianism, and argues in favour of maximizing happiness for all members of society.

In 1851 Mill married Harriet Taylor, with whom he had had a close friendship with for many years. Before marrying Mill, Taylor lived in an unhappy marriage where her husband had not only given her two children, but also syphilis. Harriet Taylor Mill's experience of marriage obviously influenced their common thoughts and ideas on the situation of married women in Victorian England. The couple read and commented on each other's writings, and there has been much debate about her role for the development of *The Subjection of Women*. Harriet Taylor no doubt had a major influence on Mill's feminism. The essay "The Enfranchisement of Women" from 1851 contains many of the same lines of argument as the later *The Subjection of Women*. We know for a fact that the short text "Enfranchisement of Women" from 1851 is from her hand. She is perhaps sharper and more radical than her husband. Harriet Taylor Mill claims that women should be accorded equality in all respects; political, civil and social. She demands equality before the law, without distinction of sex or colour of skin. Almost like an echo of Olympe de Gouges, she claims that every human being who is required to obey the law is entitled to a voice in its enactment, and every person who pays taxes to the government should be entitled to a saying in such government. Women should not only be given the right to vote, but also be considered eligible to office, Taylor Mill continues. Women must be given the chance to earn their own money and have a career for themselves. The present laws of marriage, she argues, must be re-written. Her radicalness is evident in her choice of language and metaphors. She labels the present relationship between men and women as "aristocracy of sex", claiming sex is as accidental as colour of the skin and completely irrelevant to questions of government. Moreover, she calls the division between men and women as a division into "two castes", where one is born to rule over the other. The subjection of women has no other explanation that custom and habit, she writes, it is men's physical force that lies behind this custom that now has become a tyrant.

In *The Subjection of Women* Taylor and Mill ask the rhetorical question of how suffrage could be universal while half of the human species remained excluded from it. This echoes Condorcet's writings dating a century earlier. John Stuart Mill's *On Liberty*, published in 1859, one year after Harriet's death, opens with a dedication to her and in his autobiography Mill claims that *On Liberty* was a joint production. It is therefore difficult to separate the contribution of each in the book, but as is customary I shall refer to the author of these works as "Mill".

On Liberty was published two years before *The Subjection of Women*, and it is clear that the arguments of the former infuses the latter. *On Liberty* is a defence of individual freedom. Everyone should have the freedom to pursue their own goals, Mill thinks, so long as they do not infringe on the legitimate interests of others. The advantage of this would be to enable individuals to realize their potential in their own distinctive way, which again would lead to the liberation of talents and, creativity that can benefit society. Liberty is thus good both for the individual and for society. According to Mill, recognition that women are men's equals will only bring good with it: "the removal of women's disabilities – their recognition as the equals of men in all that belongs to citizenship" (Mill, 2015: 86) will lead to a vast amount of gain for human nature. In *On The Subjection of Women* we can find passages that point directly to *On Liberty*:

> And even if we could do without them [women], would it be consistent with justice to refuse to them their fair share of honour and distinction, or to deny to them the equal moral right of all human beings to choose their occupation (short of injury to others) according to their preferences, at their own risk?
>
> (Mill, 1988: 55)

If women for some reason or other should not be given individual freedom, then this must be argued or proved accordingly, Mill argues, but no such argument exists. Both liberalist and utilitarian considerations support giving women suffrage.

John Stuart Mill strongly opposed the patriarchal family of Victorian Britain. In the 1860s, married women had virtually no rights, they could not own their own property, make contracts or a will, nor sue or be sued. They had few custody rights to their children and no legal protection against sexual or physical abuse by their husbands. It is particularly the situation of married women that occupies Mill in *On The Subjection of Women*. By marrying women enter a state of dependence that Mill compares to slavery. For Mill this dependence is worse than slavery, because "Men do not want solely the obedience of women, they want their sentiments" (ibid., 15). And as it is unlikely that women should be collectively rebellious to the power of men (ibid.), men must therefore join them in the undertaking of liberating women.

Mill's ideas were very influential. The Norwegian playwright Henrik Ibsen's wife Susanna Ibsen had read John Stuart Mill and convinced her husband to write a play on the situation of women. The result was *A Dolls' House* of 1879, which was read by the present-day as a harsh criticism of contemporary marital morals and women's lack of rights within marriage. In the play, the main character Nora has borrowed money without her husband's permission or knowledge, in order to finance a journey that later saves his life. Nora has done this out of love for her husband. But when he finds out that she has falsified her father's signature on a promissory, he does not react with love nor gratitude, but wants to send her away. Nora loses all illusions of marriage, and the play ends with the famous scene where Nora leaves her husband and children. Nora has lived a life, first as her father's pet and plaything, then as her husband's. The play illustrates how women were taught to be secondary to men, as well as the structure of the patriarchal family. The upbringing of women, that is education, culture and custom, had, according to Mill and Ibsen, made them into beings that lived for others. In modern society, Mill argued, people are no longer born to their place in life, except for women.

Much in the same way that Rousseau uncovered the origin and history of inequality between men, Mill traces the sources and development of inequality between men and women. And as mentioned Mill argues that this inequality it is not "natural". Mill thus joins the company of earlier feminist thinkers such as Poulain, Gournay, Astell, Condorcet and Wollstonecraft who all believed that it was habit, custom and culture that were responsible for women's inferior position in society. Given that the difference between men and women was not perceived as natural, it was also something that was possible to change.

In the wake of John Stuart Mill, women all over the Western world began fighting for the right to vote. Suffrage had a great symbolic value and meant that women became full members of society i.e. citizens on the same level as men. The women's suffrage movement contributed to true democracy.

Most of Mill's concerns about married women have been "solved". New legislation has changed the systematic subjection of Western women. On one point, however, Mill's ideas are still relevant for feminist theory. After arguing that male domination of women is not natural, he continues by claiming that no one can know anything definitive about the nature of women. Women have never had the possibility to develop freely, thus we cannot know what a true or natural woman is. This echoes Mary Wollstonecraft and her claim that we cannot really know what a woman actually is because until now she has only been the result of male fantasies. This idea of femininity as something unarticulated, or not yet developed, points to later feminists such as Simone de Beauvoir and Luce Irigaray, who will both be discussed in Chapter 5.

This chapter has discussed how a debate on women and equality was expanded to the area of political rights. The next chapter will explore some of the theoretical developments that followed after women won the vote.

Notes

1 One who didn't follow the law was the tragic heroine Antigone, of Sophocles' tragedy of 441 BC, who broke the law and buried her brother against her uncle king Creon's ban and prohibition. In G.W.F. Hegel's reading, the conflict between Antigone and Creon is a conflict between family and polis, between women's duties and men's duties, and the familial ethical life becomes woman's unique responsibility.

78 *Citizenship, education and the vote*

2 Condorcet hid in the house of Mme Vernet, on Rue Servadoni in Paris. While hiding here he wrote *Esquisse d'un tableau historique des progès de l'esprit humain* (*Sketch for a Historical Picture of the Progress of the Human Spirit*), posthumously published in 1795 and considered one of the major texts of the Enlightenment.
3 Charles Maurice de Talleyrand-Périgord (1754–1838) was a French politician, clergyman and diplomat. He served in several French governments and participated in the writing of *The Declaration of the Rights of Man*.

5 The difference that makes a difference

From suffrage to philosophy

The fight for women's right to vote was finally won within the first half of the 20th century: Finland introduced female suffrage in 1906, Norway in 1913, Great Britain in 1918, Germany in 1920 and France in 1945, to give a few examples. But getting the vote wasn't perhaps as transforming as women had hoped. In fact, it led to disappointment for many as the hierarchy between men and women persisted. Male was still valued over female, e.g. male literature and art were still rated as much more interesting and qualitatively better than female literature and art. Women still had to fight to be taken seriously and get access to higher positions in society. The struggle for equal opportunities was in no way over.

It is worth noting that both Virginia Woolf and Simone de Beauvoir's iconic feminist works were written just a few years after women had been given formal political rights in each of their respective countries, Great Britain and France. Virginia Woolf's *A Room of One's Own* came out in 1929, only 11 years after British women had won the vote in 1918. And Simone de Beauvoir's *The Second Sex* was published in 1949, only four years after French women got the vote. After successfully winning the vote, what was left to be said of the situation of women? What philosophical developments went into the feminist debate after the Second World War? This is what will be explored in this last chapter.

European (particularly French) philosophy in the 20th century also saw an increasing interest in difference and otherness, perhaps as a reaction to Second World War atrocities against Jews, Gypsies and people different from 'average' Europeans. The focus on otherness and equality turned in to an exploration of the flip side of equality, namely difference.[1]

This chapter will first explore Simone de Beauvoir's otherness-feminism and see how she builds on, incorporates and develops Existentialism – the philosophy of her day – into a feminist framework. The chapter will begin by having a look at difference understood as being second or secondary through the philosophical lenses of Beauvoir. The second part of the chapter investigates some of the ideas on sexual difference that arose in the wake of Beauvoir and post-structuralism, specifically those of Luce Irigaray and Judith Butler, before ending with some concluding remarks.

Woman as secondary and Other – Simone de Beauvoir

I have mentioned Simone de Beauvoir in passing in several chapters; here the focus is on what she brings to the feminist debate from her own philosophical present day i.e. Existentialism. *The Second Sex* shares many of the traits of the philosophical movement Existentialism. Existentialism is often associated with a number of thinkers in the 19th and 20th centuries who made the concrete individual central to their thought. These include thinkers as diverse as Hegel, Marx, Kierkegaard, Nietzsche, Husserl and Heidegger, and Beauvoir was influenced by all of them. A narrower use of the term "Existentialism" refers to a circle of French philosophers, where Jean-Paul Sartre figures as the central character. In the years after the Second World War, Simone de Beauvoir and Sartre became the centre of cultural and intellectual life on the left bank of Paris. Existentialism was the fashionable philosophical attitude in the 1940s and 50s, when Beauvoir and Sartre were writing their philosophical works in cafés and engaging in political controversies.

"This world has always belonged to males", Beauvoir writes in the opening of Chapter 1 in *The Second Sex* (Beauvoir, 2011). The project of the book, she says, is to investigate – in the light of existentialist philosophy – how the hierarchy of the sexes came to be. So, what is, or was existentialist philosophy? Existentialism takes as its point of departure the concrete individual, or our existence as unique individuals in concrete situations. The self is an "existing individual", an agent involved in a specific social and historical world. Existentialism's focus on "being-in-the-world" or "being-in-a-situation" becomes crucial for Beauvoir's analysis of woman in Western culture.

Existentialism was a protest against traditional and abstract philosophy in a shared belief that philosophical thinking begins with the human subject, not simply the thinking subject, the Cartesian cogito, but the living, acting, feeling, loving human individual. To understand what a human being is, it is not enough to know all the truths that natural science can tell us about, which is not to say that Existentialism denies the validity of natural science and the science of psychology. The claim is just that they are not sufficient to give a complete account of what it is to be a human being. The existentialists associated the term "existence" with the ability to reflect on one's existence, i.e. human existence. Sartre's famous dictum "existence precedes essence" means that there is no pre-given idea or account of who we are supposed to become. An individual's existence and what she or he makes out of his or her existence determines what she/he becomes. Our fate is not fixed; it is in our hands to become who we are or want to be.

According to Existentialism, there is no transcendent justification for our existence. "God is dead" and the individual is ultimately alone and unsupported in a cold and meaningless universe. No one can tell us or instruct is about the right way to live our lives. We are what we make of ourselves, our identity is defined through the choices we make in dealing with the world. Human freedom is one important pillar of Existentialism. We are always free to transform our life through our decisions. People are perhaps unaware of the extent of their freedom, but the existentialists insist that we are free to choose our own fates.

Moreover, we are embodied beings who encounter the world from the standpoint of a particular body; I am my body. Embodiment was a particularly central theme for the thinking of both Simone de Beauvoir and Maurice Merleau-Ponty. We are embodied and social beings, and as social beings we find ourselves embedded in a particular and historical context that condition our lives and determines our basic orientation towards the world. We are always embedded in a situation, we are "being-in-a-situation" or "being-in-the-world". All knowledge is situated, all inquiry must start from a situated perspective. Hence an inquiry of e.g. the situation of women must start from a woman's perspective. Even though we are embedded in a situation, we always have the ability to use our free will and transcend the situation, existentialists hold.

Simone de Beauvoir was a "professional" philosopher in the sense that she had studied philosophy and had passed exams in philosophy. She supported herself by teaching philosophy in high schools until she eventually was able to make a living as a writer. Beauvoir wrote novels, essays and philosophical treatises.

In *The Second Sex* Beauvoir wants to investigate where the submission of women comes from. She sets out to analyze all the different aspects of a woman's existence that contribute to what she calls the female condition. How will the property of being a woman affect one's life? What precise opportunities have been given to women and which ones have been denied? But, first of all, what is a woman, she asks rhetorically? Is it a person with uterus and ovaries or is there more to being a woman than just biology? Ideas of femininity and "the eternal feminine" point to something different than biology and hormones, according to Beauvoir. In her view the notion of the eternal feminine is comparable with notions of the Jewish character and the black soul – they are all notions projected on to them from an outside position. In Beauvoir's words they are all "projected as Other" – "Other" signifying contrast to a primary first. Woman is, according to Beauvoir, always understood in relationship to man, a relation that (according to her) is not symmetrical: "She determines and differentiates herself in relation to man, and he does not in relation to her; she is the inessential in front of the essential. He is the Subject he is the Absolute. She is the Other" (ibid., 6). Woman, according to Beauvoir, is Other or second to man. Her project is to uncover why is this so. Why has the world always belonged to men, she asks, something that has only recently begun to change?

Women are best suited to elucidating the situation of women, Beauvoir thinks, and this is also why her more than 700-page long critical analysis begins by stating "I am a woman". She says: "If I want to define myself, I first have to say, 'I am a woman': all other assertions will arise from this basic truth" (Beauvoir, 2011: 5). As argued in Chapter 3, this method of speaking from a first-person perspective places Beauvoir in the company of Mary Wollstonecraft as well as Marie de Gournay and Michel de Montaigne. *The Second Sex* is an inquiry of the situation or condition of women, written by one who has inside experience from the domain of inquiry. As an existentialist thinker, any critical analysis must always begin with the concrete individual. *The Second Sex* is, however, not a collection of autobiographical anecdotes. In fact, the only thing we are told about the author is this that she is a woman. *The Second Sex* begins by discussing woman from a biological, psychological and historic materialistic point of view in Book I, before discussing the lived experiences of being a woman in Book II.

After inquiring into different determining perspectives of women, and concluding that they all incorporate mythologies of femininity, Book II opens with the famous words: "One is not born, but rather becomes, woman" (ibid., 293). While Book I thoroughly analyzes all aspects that influence and shape being a woman, Book II looks into how woman is taught to assume her condition, how she experiences this and how she can escape this condition, i.e. how she can liberate herself. Existentialist philosophy holds that we are responsible for our own lives, for what we make of the possibilities given to us, and how we live and develop as individual beings. Given all the constraints woman has been shown in *The Second Sex* to live under, how can she still realize her full potential as an individual, as a subject, without consideration of her sex? Perhaps Simone de Beauvoir herself and her unconventional life are the best answer to that.

Beauvoir's *Second Sex* presents two main thoughts or arguments. Firstly, one is not born but rather becomes woman. Secondly, culture makes woman into the Other, by which she means that there is more to being a woman than just biology. Regarding the existentialist imperative to take responsibility for one's own life, it might appear to some readers of Beauvoir that this is a next to impossible task for women given all the constraints and barriers pointed out in *The Second Sex*. But, as Beauvoir has shown there is nothing natural in femininity; femininity ought not to determine or frame a woman's life. The reason why it does, however, is due to culture, not nature, and here we might remember the arguments of the earlier Poulain. One is not born, but rather becomes woman, Beauvoir famously wrote. Thus, she also writes that today's woman is not nature's creation. There are no transcendent or pre-destined notions of what a woman is, but woman's lack of freedom prevents her from becoming man's equal. The free woman is just being born, Beauvoir writes. Beauvoir never concludes that man and woman are identical, rather she holds that physical weakness makes woman vulnerable and disposes her to passivity.

According to Beauvoir, the body is a situation. Men's and women's bodies are different, thus a woman's relation to her own body, the male body and pregnancy is different from man's relation to his body, the female body and pregnancy (ibid., 782). This bodily difference is a difference that makes a difference. In order to emancipate woman, one has to refuse to enclose her to these relations. Beauvoir's ideal is a transformation of woman, the birth of a new woman. Put in other words, she dreams of realizing the Enlightenment's idea of universal human rights. The idea of universal human rights does not operate with primary and secondary subjects, the aim of universal human rights is to treat everyone as equals.

While all previous feminists agitate for women in plural, Beauvoir's object of analysis is the singular woman. This is likely in order to produce a more general account. Although some of her descriptions and analyses are taken from the context of post-war Paris, others are remarkably general, which also explains why *The Second Sex* has been translated into as diverse languages as Chinese, Russian and Persian, and continues to be important and relevant for women all over the world. Simone de Beauvoir's *The Second Sex* has given feminism a solid theoretical framework and a vocabulary to continue to work from. The book has subsequently been referred to as a "feminist Bible".

Simone de Beauvoir was followed by the feminists of the 1970s, the Women's Lib. By this time women entered academia in large numbers. For many it was *The Second Sex* that paved the way for the radical changes that occurred in the 70s. Toril Moi, author of an intellectual biography on Simone de Beauvoir, *The Making of an Intellectual Woman* (2002) claims that Beauvoir became the leading feminist thinker and emblematic intellectual woman of the 20th century. Moi's biography reveals how difficult it was for Beauvoir, and still is for women, to be taken seriously as intellectuals.

It would be an over-simplification to call Beauvoir an equality-feminist, but she is certainly not a sexual difference-feminist like Luce Irigaray and Judith Butler; that is why I at the beginning of this chapter called her an otherness-feminist. Equality-feminism seeks to establish the equality of the sexes in all domains focusing on the basic similarities between men and women. For Beauvoir women are equal to men in relevant respects, but also different in other respects – her point being that such (bodily) differences – should not necessarily make them secondary to men.

Sexual difference as a philosophical problem – Luce Irigaray

In the previous chapters we have seen how equality has been the object of feminist reflection ever since the writings of Marie de Gournay in the 16th century. We shall now have a closer look at the writings of a thinker who twists the discussion and claims that *sexual difference* is what we have to think through. According to Luce Irigaray, the equality challenge can only be solved by exploring women's difference to men and how this difference is thought of and understood.

Irigaray can be placed under the heading post-structuralism, which is mainly a term for French philosophy after structuralism. As a movement in philosophy, post-structuralism arose in the wake of 1968 and is characterized by its effort to think "difference" in another way than previous philosophy. The theme of difference is fundamental for all post-structuralists, including Gilles Deleuze, Jacques Derrida and Jean-François Lyotard, and what they respectively term *difference, différance* and the *differend*. They are all wary of thought that reduces diversity to sameness by unifying concepts or theories. For feminist thinkers like Luce Irigaray, Julia Kristeva and Hélène Cixous it is *sexual difference* that is their theoretical point of departure. Cixous, writer and literary critic is famous for what she calls *écrtiture feminine* (female writing), a genre of writing that deviates from traditional masculine styles of writing examining female and bodily experiences, claims that what is lacking in literature is exploration of female sexuality and desire. Luce Irigaray on her side claims that a female subject position is what is lacking or absent in philosophy. Any theory of the subject as a universal entity hides in reality false masculine subject, Irigaray argues. This false universalization erases the difference women represent. The blame for this is put on *fallogocentrism*, a term coined by Derrida to refer to the privileging of the masculine (phallus) and logos in construction of meaning, which accordingly has served as compass needle in philosophy for decades. This exclusion of the female has the fatal consequence that women lack an adequate language to express specific female experiences, or saying what being a woman involves, in French also termed *parler femme*, i.e. speak as a woman. In the previous chapter I suggested that Mary Wollstonecraft and John Stuart Mill perhaps had something in common with post-structuralist feminism when they claimed that one cannot know anything definitive about the nature of women because they had never had the possibility of developing and expressing themselves freely. To my ears this sounds like an early version of *parler femme* or *écrtiture feminine*.

Luce Irigaray was born in Belgium in 1932 but lives and works in Paris. Her thinking is controversial and has been the object of debate among feminists and philosophers for several decades. Her writing is also at times quite opaque and at times challenging to interpret. The book *Speculum* from 1974, which was also her PhD thesis, got her expelled from the famous analyst Jacques Lacan's seminars. Even though she was trained in psychology, Irigaray insists on being read as a *philosopher*. She operates in the margins of philosophy, where sexual difference is her major philosophical concern. By "margins" of philosophy I mean that the topic she writes about, as well as writing style and method, are all rather untraditional. In some of her works she constructs imaginary dialogues with prominent philosophers e.g. Plato, Aristotle, Descartes, Spinoza, Heidegger and Nietzsche. In her book on Nietzsche, *Amante Marin* (*Marine Lover*) she engages herself in a fantasy love affair with the philosopher. Through an amorous dialogue with the male philosopher she interrogates Nietzsche's thinking and tries to explore how sexual difference is absent in his philosophy. As pointed out in Chapter 1 it is conspicuous that she never applies her innovative re-readings of the history of philosophy to any woman philosopher from the past. However, what makes Irigaray controversial for some feminists is the fact that she maximizes sexual difference rather than minimizing it.

Sexual difference is according to Irigaray the most basic difference and background of experience in a human's life. But sexual difference is also a blind spot in philosophy, she thinks. Comparable to how Heidegger claimed that *being* was what philosophy had forgot to think about Irigaray claims that sexual difference is what still needs to be thought through. In reality sexual difference does not exist, she claims, since women's subject position, so far, has not been given a voice in Western culture. Philosophy has taken for granted for example that a universalizing of the subject is possible, while Irigaray claims that the traditional subject of philosophy is in reality male and that the theories of philosophy, regardless in ethics, epistemology or aesthetics wrongfully present the experiences of men as universal while simultaneously devaluating female experiences. We think that philosophy is gender-neutral, while in realty it is very gendered, she claims. Genevieve Lloyd describes Irigaray's contributions to philosophy this way:

> The work of Luce Irigaray has been influential in the development of strategies directed to the identification within philosophical texts of "speaking positions" which while supposedly gender-neutral, incorporate assumptions of maleness.
>
> (Lloyd, 2006: 246)

Irigaray also thinks that the rhetoric of liberal feminism has a propensity to exalt man and the masculine to an ideal. She thus aims is to find a way of thinking and understanding sexual difference that is neither dichotomous nor hierarchical. Rather than campaigning for equality with men she urges us to question what it is that woman wants to be equal to. The only way in which the status of women could be altered fundamentally is by a powerful female symbolic to represent the female side of sexual difference. What is at stake is the ethical, ontological, and social status of women, she writes. Equality-feminism reduces women to men, she thinks, the challenge is rather to find ways of how to respect women's difference. Exactly what this difference is or entails, however, she never says or refers to, but insists that her focus is on the *possibility* of a female subject position, exploring where, when or how femininity could be articulated. She refuses to give a definition of woman, insisting that women must give it to themselves.

Part of Irigaray's argument follows in the footsteps of Jacques Derrida's (and before him Nietzsche's) critique of Western metaphysics as built on binary oppositions. For Irigaray it is pressing to conceive of man and woman as different, but not as opposites. To overcome the idea of sexual difference as dichotomous is crucial in order to overcome gender hierarchy, as opposition and hierarchy are closely embedded. In *Genealogy of Morals*, Nietzsche writes that "different from" has somehow in the course of history changed meaning to "worse than". At the heart of Irigaray's thinking lies the question: how can we think or conceive of sexual difference without reducing it to a question of dichotomy or hierarchy? She shares with other French difference-thinkers the idea that Western culture hasn't yet managed to genuinely think difference at all. Difference has in her view so far only been understood as another version of the Same, a mirroring of the One, as either complement, lack or negation. For Irigaray the question thus becomes how to think woman without reducing her to a reflection of man. The equality discourse has brought us as far as it possibly can, but no further, she claims. Given that women's difference works as justificatory ground for their lower social status, the solution to the problem of gender hierarchy cannot be found in simply neglecting these differences. In order to solve the problem of gender hierarchy one rather needs to rethink what sexual difference is and evaluate what is specifically feminine. Those who insist that "women can do anything men can do" tends to leave male-dominated and biased ideas and values unquestioned. In fact, the problem is exactly the absence of alternatives to these values. For Irigaray what needs changing is just as much culture, society and politics, not just women. Her thinking represents a move from "fixing the women" to "fixing the culture and system". She even thinks it is a mistake for women to demand equality, to demand equality presupposes a point of comparison, or an already settled unquestionable norm, in her view.

> To whom or to what do women want to be equalized? To men? To a salary? To a public office? To what standard? Why no to themselves?
> (Irigaray, 1993: 12)

Again, we see that the point for Irigaray is that woman is not just equal to man, but also fundamentally and radically different. Irigaray's focus on sexual difference has raised suspicion about return to the old idealization of the "eternal feminine" and she has more than once been accused of unwarranted essentialism, which has been hotly debated among scholars. Essentialism is best described as the view that human traits like male and female have an innate existence or universal validity rather than being a social, ideological or intellectual construct. In my own view she is not *defining* woman but is rather theorizing about the *feminine*. In order to construct a positive representation of the feminine she searches for new linguistic tools, and this experimenting with language is what often makes readers interpret her as an essentialist.[2] Anti-essentialism has played an important role and been a big issue in recent feminist theory. But for

Irigaray, a move towards neutral sex just conceals once more a masculine privilege and norm.

A somewhat related focus on difference can be found in feminist care ethics, e.g. in psychologist Carol Gilligan's work *In a Different Voice* from 1982. Men and women tend to view morality in different terms, Gilligan writes. Women thus emphasize empathy and compassion, i.e. care, over justice-based ethical approaches, or consequentialist theories. In Gilligan's view there is an "ethics of care" in women's moral reasoning. Like Luce Irigaray, Gilligan's theories have been criticized for reinforcing traditional stereotypes of women. While I do not want to pass judgement on either Irigaray's or Gilligan's theories, I think much of the critique misses their joint concern for giving a positive articulation of what has traditionally been associated with women and femininity.

Even though Beauvoir sometimes is termed as an equality-feminist and Irigaray as a difference-feminist they both take as their point of departure the *condition* of women. Beauvoir examines under what existential philosophical conditions women have lived and live their lives. Irigaray on the other hand examines the linguistic and philosophical conditions under which it is possible to articulate femininity, or this sex that is not male, at all. How is sexual difference possible within philosophy?

Feminist arguments seem to develop through a dialectics of equality and difference. Equality and difference are the two core concepts and ideas underlying all modern feminist thought. If modern feminism began as a discussion on equality with Gournay in 1642, it ends, until now, with Luce Irigaray's focus on and philosophizing of sexual difference. Feminist thinking alternates between placing equality or difference as a foundation and base to reflect from. Although many of these theories from the outset come across as quite divergent, we can nonetheless conclude that a common milestone for all of them is to arrive at a position from which to claim that men and women are equal, but different.

The trouble with gender – Judith Butler

Before ending this intellectual journey of feminist thinking, I suggest a last stop to visit elements of Judith Butler's feminist writings. In her ground-breaking work *Gender Trouble* from 1990, Judith Butler openly acknowledges her debt to Beauvoir and Irigaray. But contrary to the latter two, Butler is not so much concerned with the specific question of what a woman is, rather she is concerned with who the subject of feminism is as well as exploring what gender as such is – regardless whether female, male, or non-binary, and what the relationship between sex and gender is.

In recent decades much feminist theory has relied upon the conceptual distinction between sex and gender, where sex points to biology and nature, and gender to culture and society. The sex/gender divide is by many regarded as a re-writing of Beauvoir's famous "one is not born, but rather becomes, woman". However, such a reading has been challenged and criticized, e.g. by Sara Heinämaa who claims that Simone de Beauvoir's *The Second Sex* has mistakenly been interpreted as a theory of gender.[3]

In *Gender Trouble* Judith Butler presents a harsh radical critique of the notion of gender and all feminism that is built on this concept. The term "gender" is a 20th century linguistic innovation and originates from the 1960s where it was first used to explain transvestite behaviour. Butler argues that sex (male, female) is seen to cause gender (masculine, feminine), which in turn is seen to cause desire towards the other sex. But for Butler gender does not follow causally from sex, nor is it determined by sex.

While Butler acknowledges that the concept of gender gives a good starting point to argue against biological determinism, she also believes that it presupposes a heterosexual norm. This hidden norm is what Butler sets out to expose and criticize. She thus walks in the footsteps of Descartes and the project of overcoming habitual thinking. Gender is for Butler conditioned by more than the sex/gender divide; our understanding of man and woman presupposes according to her a heterosexual norm. Being a woman is a much more complex phenomenon than feminism hitherto has grasped. The only setting in which woman can be understood as a stable and coherent category is within a heterosexual matrix, Butler thinks. In her view, even if we make a distinction between sex and gender, we are still left with the question of why women become female and men male. If there was a causal relation between sex and gender then biological innate structures would determine interests, behaviour and identity. But gender is nothing but cultural interpretations of sex differences, Butler argues. So, to explain why women become female and men become male, she introduces her theory of performativity and thereby rejects the supposed causal links between sex and gender. For Butler, gender is not something a person is or has, but something a person does, gender is connected to performativity and doing. Gender, she writes "is a kind of doing, an incessant activity performed, in part, without one's knowing and without one's willing" (Butler, 2004: 1). For Butler the seeming naturalness of being female is constituted through performative acts. Certain heterosexual configurations of gender have seized hegemonic hold, she writes, but queer sexual orientation can destabilize gender and work subversively. Woman cannot be given ontological status but is rather a free-floating category. For Butler, sex and gender are equally cultural products and the one cannot follow from the other, they are both culturally constructed. In the beginning of *Gender Trouble* she writes:

> The relation between masculine and feminine cannot be represented in a signifying economy in which the masculine constitutes the closed circle of signifier and signified. Paradoxically enough, Beauvoir prefigured this impossibility in *The Second Sex* when she argued that men could not settle the question of women because they would then be acting as both judge and party to the case.
>
> (Butler, 1990: 11)

However, the claim that men cannot settle the question of women because they would then be both judge and party is not Beauvoir's argument, but Beauvoir citing Poulain de la Barre. Remember how Beauvoir alluded and gave tribute to Poulain on the title-page of *The Second Sex*. Nonetheless, Butler takes this claim as critical for arguing that a rethinking of feminism is necessary. Who is the subject of feminism, Butler asks rhetorically? For according to her, feminism has no pre-given subject. Rather, feminism produces the category of women, which it again claims to represent and thereafter offers to liberate. The problem with the circularity of the feminine and the masculine is that it is a masculine construction, and moreover a heteronormative construction. Heterosexuality makes sex differences appear natural, Butler writes. The heterosexual matrix is an invisible norm that comes through as natural, until challenged. This norm is also dominant within feminism, Butler claims, while she on her part wishes to broaden the feminist theorization by bringing sexuality to the debate. There is more to woman or femininity than sex/gender, it is rather better understood as sex/gender/sexuality.

This heterosexual matrix has affinity in Mary Wollstonecraft's writings, discussed in Chapter 4. Wollstonecraft held that what had been written so far on women had primarily been written by men, and secondly written with the goal of making women alluring mistresses rather than affectionate wives and rational mothers. She seems to share with Butler the idea that gender hierarchy is lending male heterosexual desire a hand.

The point here is not to examine Butler's theory and argument in depth, nor argue in favour or against it, but rather to show that she also builds upon arguments that are much older than what appears from her writing. Butler's post-structuralist theory has roots in an Early

Modern Cartesianism. I think Butler here is an example of what was pointed to in the Introduction; a feminist tendency to forget or ignore its own historicity and consider itself as oriented towards the present. A historical consciousness will prevent us from having to "invent the wheel" all over again and starting from year zero. Contextualization and dialogue with the past offer, to my mind, a richer framing to a discussion. But it would be futile to criticize Butler for not knowing that Beauvoir is referring to Poulain, as this reference was omitted in the first English translation of *The Second Sex*.

My point is simply that some feminists from the past had similar ideas as Judith Butler. Butler's question about whether there is a causal relation between sex and gender might seem to echo Elisabeth of Bohemia's question to Descartes concerning the relationship and causality between body and mind. What is the relation between body-sex-nature on the one hand and mind-gender-culture on the other? Is the relation between the two a binary opposition, a contradiction or dichotomy, or are they more intertwined than what first appears? As we have seen in the previous chapters, several feminists through history have argued in different ways that the understanding of women is based on culture rather than nature. Perhaps without knowing it Butler bases some of her discussion on an issue that has occupied feminist thinkers for centuries, namely the cultural construction of gender. Modern vocabulary makes it sound like a recent one. But, as we saw in Chapter 3, Poulain de la Barre exposed the inferiority of women as a cultural construction, and one that is very similar to what is understood by gender, or sex/gender.

This chapter discussed three feminist thinkers who in various ways have advocated a difference that makes a difference. Beauvoir's idea of women's otherness, Irigaray's idea of sexual difference and Butler's idea of hetero/homosexual difference all point to phenomena that shape the lives of women (and men).

Notes

1 Emmanuel Lévinas' idea of "the face of the other", Simone de Beauvoir's idea of "woman as secondary and other", and Theodore Adorno's idea of "radical otherness" are all examples of this philosophical vogue.
2 Toril Moi e.g. has argued that her thinking entails essentialism (Moi, 1985: 142).
3 According to Heinämaa, interpreters have failed to adequately to understand Beauvoir's aims. In her view, Beauvoir is not trying to explain facts, events, or states of affairs, but to reveal, unveil, or uncover meanings of woman, female, and feminine. Instead of a theory, Heinämaa claims, Beauvoir's book presents a phenomenological description of the sexual difference (Heinämaa, 1997).

Concluding remarks

This book is in no way exhaustive. There are obviously many other ways of telling the history of feminism than the one I have chosen. My aim has been to present feminism as an inherent part of Modernity and demonstrate and make visible a philosophical continuity of thought. By discussing historical examples of feminist thinkers, I have tried to illustrate that feminism is a tradition of thought in its own right. Seeing feminism as a larger enterprise, and not small isolated attempts here and there by daring and exceptional individuals, will give us a more coherent understanding of how different developments that has taken place.

While many feminists criticize the history of philosophy, in particular Descartes' philosophy, for gendering reason and objectivity as male, I have tried to show that a different story can be told. I have wanted to show how the history of philosophy has been, and still is, a source for the advancement of feminism, even the philosophy of Descartes. The aim of the book has been to follow the developments of mainstream philosophical arguments and thereby reveal the parallel or dynamic development in feminist thought. In addition, I have tried to establish connections between contemporary feminist theory and the history of feminism. I have not only tried to uncover the history of feminist thought and its relevance for contemporary feminist thinking, but also tried to bring feminist voices from the past and present into a dialogue. My aim has not been to give thorough introductions to all these feminist thinkers, other books have to be consulted for that purpose. The contribution of this book, I hope, is rather to connect feminist thinking to the canon of European intellectual history. Feminism is not something in the margins of European culture, but right at the heart of it. One benefit of a historical consciousness for feminism is to realize how long it has taken to get where we are today; another one is to see all the different steps and contributions that were necessary for its development until the present status quo.

Bibliography

Ahmed, Sara. "Killing Joy: Feminism and the History of Happiness". In *Signs: Journal of Women in Culture and Society*, Vol. 35, No. 3, 2010.

Akkerman, Tjitske and Siep Stuurman (eds.). *Perspectives on Feminist Political Thought in European History: From the Middle Ages to the Present*. London and New York: Routledge, 1998.

Assman, Aleida. "Canon and Archive", page 106. In Erll, Astrid and Ansgar Nünning, (eds.). *Cultural Memory Studies*. Berlin and New York: Walter de Gruyter, 2008.

Astell, Mary. *A Serious Proposal to the Ladies* [1694]. Edited by Patricia Springborg. Peterborough: Broadview Press, 2002.

Barker, Chris. *Cultural Studies. Theory and Practice*. London: Sage Publications, 2000.

Bauer, Nancy. *Simone de Beauvoir, Philosophy, & Feminism*. New York: Columbia University Press, 2001.

Beauvoir, Simone de. *After the War: Force of Circumstance, 1944–1952* [1965]. New York: Marlowe & Co, Paragon House, 1994.

Beauvoir, Simone de. *The Second Sex* [1949]. Translated by Constance Borde and Sheila Malovany-Chevalier. London: Vintage Books, 2011.

Benhabib, Seyla. "Feminism and the Question of Postmodernism". In *Situating the Self*. Cambridge: Polity Press, 1992.

Bergès, Sandrine. *Wollstonecraft's A Vindication of the Rights of Woman*. London: Routledge, 2013.

Berlin, Isaiah. *The Sense of Reality*. New York: Farrar, Straus and Giroux, 1998.

Bocaccio, Giovanni. *Famous Women*. Cambridge, MA: Harvard University Press, 2001.

Bordo, Susan. *The Flight to Objectivity: Essays on Cartesianism and Culture*. New York: State University of New York Press, 1987.

Broad, Jacqueline and Karen Green. *A History of Women's Political Thought in Europe*. Cambridge: Cambridge University Press, 2009.

Broad, Jacqueline. *Women Philosophers of the Seventeenth Century*. Cambridge: Cambridge University Press, 2002.

Bibliography

Butler, Judith. *Frames of War: When Is Life Grievable?*London and New York: Verso, 2009.
Butler, Judith. *Gender Trouble: Feminism and the Subversion of Identity*. New York and London: Routledge, 1990.
Butler, Judith. *Undoing Gender*. New York: Routledge, 2004.
Cajori, Florian. *A History of Mathematical Notations*. New York: Dover Publications, Inc., 1993.
Chappell, Vere. *The Cambridge Companion to John Locke*. Cambridge: Cambridge University Press, 1994.
Cixous, Hélène. *The Hélène Cixous Reader*. With a preface by Hélène Cixous and a foreword by Jacques Derrida. Edited by Susan Sellers. London: Routledge, 2003.
Condorcet, Marquis de. *Political Writings*, edited by Lukes, Steven and Nadia Urbinati. Cambridge: Cambridge University Press, 2012.
Cott, Nancy F. *The Grounding of Modern Feminism*. New Haven and London: Yale University Press, 1987.
Cottingham, John (ed.). *The Cambridge Companion to Descartes*. Cambridge: Cambridge University Press, 1999.
Davis, Natalie Zemon. *Women on the Margins: Three Seventeenth-century Lives*. Cambridge, MA: Harvard University Press, 1995.
Descartes, René. *Discourse on the Method*. Translated by Ian MacLean. Oxford: Oxford University Press, 2008.
Descartes, René. *Meditations on First Philosophy*. Edited by John Cottingham with an introductory essay by Bernard Williams. Cambridge: Cambridge University Press, 1996.
Doeuff, Michèle le. *The Philosophical Imaginary*. Stanford, California: Stanford University Press, 1989.
Elisabeth of Bohemia. *The Correspondence between Princess Elisabeth of Bohemia and René Descartes (The Other Voice in Early Modern Europe)*. Edited and translated by Lisa Shapiro. Chicago & London: The University of Chicago Press, 2007.
Fairchilds, Cissie. *Women in Early Modern Europe 1500–1700*. Harlow: Pearson Longman, 2007.
Falco, Maria J. (ed.). *Feminist Interpretations of Mary Wollstonecraft*. Pennsylvania: The Pennsylvania State University Press, 1996.
Frankel, Lois. "Damaris Cudworth Masham: A Seventeenth Century Feminist Philosopher". In *Hypatia*, Vol. 4, No. 1, Spring 1989.
Fraser, Nancy. "Feminist Politics in the Age of Recognition: A Two-Dimensional Approach to Gender Justice". In *Studies in Social Justice*, Vol. 1, No. 1, Winter 2007.
Gilligan, Carol. *In a Different Voice. Psychological Theory and Women's Development*. Harvard: Harvard University Press, 2016.
Gournay, Marie de. *Apology for the Woman Writing and Other Works* (The Other Voice in Early Modern Europe). Edited and with an introduction by Richard Hillman, Translated by Colette Quesnel. Chicago: University of Chicago Press, 2002.

Bibliography 95

Grosz, Elizabeth. *Volatile Bodies: Towards a Corporeal Feminism*. Bloomington: Indiana University Press, 1994.

Habermas, Jürgen. *The Philosophical Discourse of Modernity*. Translated by Frederick Lawrence, Cambridge: Polity Press, 1987.

Hajdin, Mane. "Introduction" in *The Notion of Equality*. Edited by Mane Hajdin. Aldershot, Burlington USA, Singapore, Sydney: Ashgate, 2001.

Harth, Erica. *Cartesian Women: Versions and Subversions of Rational Discourse in the Old Regime (Reading Women Writing)*. New York: Cornell University Press, 1992.

Haslanger, Sally and Nancy Tuana. Stanford Online Encyclopedia of Philosophy: https://plato.stanford.edu/archives/sum2012/entries/feminism-topics.

Hays, Mary. *Memoirs of Emma Courtney* [1759]. Oxford: Oxford University Press, 2009.

Heinämaa, Sara. "What is a Woman? Butler and Beauvoir on the Foundations of the Sexual Difference". In *Hypatia*, Vol. 12: 1997, page 20–39.

Ilsley, Marjory Henry. *A Daughter of the Renaissance: Marie le Jars de Gournay: Her Life and Works*. The Hague: Mouton & Co., 1963.

Irigaray, Luce. *je, tu, nous. Towards a Culture of Difference*. Translated by Alison Martin. New York and London: Routledge, 1993.

Irigaray, Luce. *Speculum of the Other Woman*. Translated by Gillian C. Gill. Ithaca, New York: Cornell University Press, 1985.

Irwin, Joyce L. "Anna Maria van Schurman and Her Intellectual Circle" in Anna Maria van Schurman. *Whether a Christian Woman Should be Educated (and Other Writings from her Intellectual Circle)*, The Other Voice in Early Modern Europe Series. Chicago and London: The University of Chicago Press, 1998.

Israel, Jonathan. *A Revolution of the Mind: Radical Enlightenment and the Intellectual Origins of Modern Democracy*. Princeton: Princeton University Press, 2010.

Israel, Jonathan. *Enlightenment Contested: Philosophy, Modernity, and the Emancipation of Man 1670–1752*. Oxford: Oxford University Press, 2006.

Jaggar, Alison. "On Sexual Equality". In *Ethics*, Vol. 84, No. 4, 1974.

Jaggar, Alison. *Just Methods: An Interdisciplinary Feminist Reader*. Boulder and London: Paradigm Publishers, 2008.

Jensen, Anne E. *Holberg og kvinderne eller Et forsvar for ligeretten*. Copenhagen: Gyldendal, 1984.

Johnson, Claudia L. "Introduction" in *The Cambridge Companion to Mary Wollstonecraft*, edited by Claudia L. Johnson. Cambridge: Cambridge University Press, 2002.

Jolley, Nicholas. "The reception of Descartes' philosophy". In John Cottingham (ed.). *The Cambridge Companion to Descartes*. Cambridge: Cambridge University Press, 1992.

Kelly, Joan. "Did Women Have a Renaissance?" in Joan Kelly. *Women, History, and Theory*. Chicago: University of Chicago Press, 1984.

96 Bibliography

Kelly, Joan. "Early Feminist Theory and the Querelle des Femmes". In *Signs*, Vol. 8, No 1, Autumn, 1982.
Knott, Sarah and Barbara Taylor (eds.). *Women, Gender and Enlightenment*. Houndsmills, Basingstoke, Hampshire: Palgrave Macmillan, 2005.
Kristeva, Julia. "Women's Time" in *The Kristeva Reader*. Edited by Toril Moi. Oxford: Basil Blackwell Ltd., 1986.
Lanser, Susan. *Fictions of Authority*. Ithaca and London: Cornell University Press, 1992.
Lloyd, Genevieve. "Feminism in history of philosophy. Appropriating the past". In Fricker, Miranda and Jennifer Hornsby (eds.). *The Cambridge Companion to Feminism in Philosophy*. Cambridge: Cambridge University Press, 2000.
Lloyd, Genevieve. "The Power of Spinoza: Feminist Conjunctions". Susan James interviews Genevieve Lloyd and Moira Gatens. In *Hypatia*, Vol. 15, No. 2, 2000.
Lloyd, Genevieve. *The Man of Reason: "Male" and "Female" in Western Philosophy*. London: Routledge, 1984.
Locke, John. *Two Treatises of Government*. Cambridge: Cambridge University Press, 1988.
Maclean, Ian. *Woman Triumphant: Feminism in French Literature 1610–1652*. Oxford: Oxford University Press, 1977.
Martinich, A.P., Fritz Allhof and Anand Jayprakash Vaidya. *Early Modern Philosophy: Essential Readings with Commentary*. "General Introduction" by A. P. Martinich. Malden, Oxford, Victoria: Blackwell Publishing, 2007.
Masham, Damaris. *Occasional Thoughts. In reference to a Virtuous or Christian Life* [1705]. Reprinted in Great Britain by Amazon.com.
Melehy, Hassan. *Writing Cogito: Montaigne, Descartes and the Institution of the Modern Subject*. New York: State University of New York Press, 1997.
Mill, Harriet Taylor. "Enfranchisement of Women" [1851], in *The Complete Works of Harriet Taylor Mill*. Indiana: Indiana University Press, 1998.
Mill, John Stuart. *On Liberty* [1859]. Oxford: Oxford University Press, 2015.
Mill, John Stuart. *The Subjection of Women* [1869]. Edited by Susan Moller Okin. Indiana, Indianapolis: Hackett Publishing Company, Inc., 1988.
Mitchell, P. M. "Introduction" in Ludvig Holberg: *Moral Reflections & Epistles*. Edited and translated by P.M. Mitchell. Norwich: Norvik Press, 1991.
Moi, Toril. *Sexual/Textual Politics: Feminist Literary Theory*. New York and London: Routledge, 1985.
Moi, Toril. *Simone de Beauvoir: The Making of an Intellectual Woman*. Oxford: Oxford University Press, 2009.
Moi, Toril. *What Is a Woman?: And Other Essays*. Oxford: Oxford University Press, 2001.
Montaigne, Michel de. *The Complete Essays*. Translated by M. A. Screech. London: Penguin Classics, 2003.
Nietzsche, Friedrich. *On the Genealogy of Morality*. Introduction by Keith Ansell-Pearson. Translated by Carol Diethe. Cambridge: Cambridge University Press, 2006.

Nochlin, Linda. "Why Have There Been No Great Woman Artists?" in Thomas B. Hess and Elizabeth C. Baker. *Art and Sexual Politics*. New York: Collier Books, Macmillian Publishing Company, 1971.

O'Neill, Eileen. "Disappearing Ink: Early Modern Women Philosophers and Their Fate in History" in Janet Kournay (ed.). *Philosophy in a Feminist Voice: Critiques and Reconstructions*. Princeton, New Jersey: Princeton University Press, 1997.

O'Neill, Eileen. "Justifying the Inclusion of Women in Our Histories of Philosophy" in Linda Martín Alcoff and Eva Feder Kittay. *The Blackwell Guide to Feminist Philosophy*. Blackwell Publishing Ltd., 2007.

Offen, Karen. *European Feminisms 1700–1950*. Stanford, California: Stanford University Press, 2000.

Okin, Susan Moller. *Women in Western Political Thought*. Princeton, New Jersey: Princeton University Press, 1992.

Owesen, Ingeborg W. *Sexual Difference as a Philosophical Problem: The Philosophies, Styles and Methods of Luce Irigaray and Friedrich Nietzsche*. PhD thesis. Oslo: Faculty of Humanities, University of Oslo, 2008.

Poulain de la Barre, François. *On the Equality of the Two Sexes in Three Cartesian Feminist Treatises*. Introductions and Annotations by Marcelle Maistre Welch. Translated by Vivien Bosley. Chicago and London: The University of Chicago Press, 2002.

Rendall, Jane. *The Origins of Modern Feminism*. Basingstoke: Macmillan, 1985.

Rorty, Richard. "The historiography of philosophy: four genres" in Richard Rorty, Schneewind and Skinner. *Philosophy in History*. Cambridge: Cambridge University Press, 1984.

Rousseau, Jean-Jacques. *Émile, or On Education* [1762]. Translated by Barbara Foxley. London: Penguin Classics, 2007.

Rousseau, Jean-Jacques. *The Social Contract and Discourses* [1762]. Everyman's Library, translation and introduction by G.D.H. Cole. London: J.M. Dent & Sons Ltd, 1993.

Rubin, Miri. "The languages of late-medieval feminism" in Akkerman, Tjitske and Siep Stuurman (eds.). *Perspectives on Feminist Political Thought in European History*. London and New York: Routledge, 1998.

Schott, Robin May. "Feminism and the History of Philosophy" in Linda Alcoff and Eva Kittay (eds.). *Feminist Philosophy*. Oxford: Blackwell Publishing, 2007.

Schurman, Anna Maria van. *Whether a Christian Woman Should be Educated – and other writings from her intellectual life*. Edited and translated by Joyce L. Irwin. Chicago: The University of Chicago Press, 1998.

Scott, Joan Wallach. *Only Paradoxes to Offer: French Feminists and the Rights of Man*. Harvard: Harvard University Press, 1996.

Sen, Amartya. "Equality of what? (Lecture delivered at Stanford University, 22 May 1979)", in MacMurrin, Sterling M. (ed.), *The Tanner Lectures on Human Values* (1st ed.), Salt Lake City, Utah: University of Utah Press, 1980.

Bibliography

Sen, Amartya. *The Idea of Justice*. London: Penguin Books, 2010.
Skinner, Quentin (ed.). *Philosophy in History*. Cambridge: Cambridge University Press, 1984.
Skinner, Quentin. *Liberty Before Liberalism*. Cambridge: Cambridge University Press, 1998.
Springborg, Patricia. "Introduction" in Mary Astell. *A Serious Proposal to the Ladies*. Edited by Patricia Springborg. Mississauga, Canada: Broadview Press, 2002.
Stuurman, Siep. "The Canon of the History of Political Thought: Its Critique and a Proposed Alternative" *History and Theory*, Vol. 39, May 2000.
Stuurman, Siep. *François Poulain de la Barre and the Invention of Modern Equality*. Cambridge, Massachusetts: Harvard University Press, 2004.
Taylor, Barbara. *Mary Wollstonecraft and the Feminist Imagination*. Cambridge: Cambridge University Press, 2003.
Taylor, Charles. "Philosophy and its history" in Richard Rorty, Schneewind and Skinner. *Philosophy in History*. Cambridge: Cambridge University Press, 1984.
Vintges, Karen. "Beauvoir's philosophy as the hidden paradigm of contemporary feminism" in Akkerman, Tjitske and Siep Stuurman (eds.). *Perspectives on Feminist Political Thought in European History*. London and New York: Routledge, 1998.
Waithe, Mary Ellen (ed.). *A History of Women Philosophers* vol. 1-4, Dordrecht, Boston, Lancaster: Martinus Nijhoff Publishers, 1987-1995.
Waldron, Jeremy. *God, Locke and Equality: Christian Foundations in Locke's Political Thought*. Cambridge: Cambridge University Press, 2002.
Wilkin, Rebecca M. *Women, Imagination and the Search for Truth in Early Modern France*. Hampshire, England: Ashgate, 2008.
Williams, Bernard. "Introductory Essay" in *Descartes: Meditations on First Philosophy*. Edited by John Cottingham. Cambridge: Cambridge University Press, 1996.
Williams, Bernard. *Problems of the Self – Philosophical Papers 1956-1972: "The idea of equality"*. Cambridge: Cambridge University Press, 1973.
Williams, David. *Condorcet and Modernity*. Cambridge: Cambridge University Press, 2004.
Wollstonecraft, Mary. *Letters Written in Sweden, Norway and Denmark* [1796]. Edited by Tone Brekke and Jon Mee. Oxford: Oxford University Press, 2009.
Wollstonecraft, Mary. *Vindication of the Rights of Woman* [1792]. Edited by Sylvana Tomaselli. Cambridge: Cambridge University Press, 1995.
Woolf, Virginia. *A Room of One's Own and Three Guineas* [1929]. Oxford World Classics. Oxford: Oxford University Press, 2008.

Index

Adorno, Theodore 91
Afghanistan War 15
Africa 9
Agrippa, Cornelius 27
Ahmed, Sara 17, 18
Akkerman, Tjitske 26, 43
American Revolution 62
androcentrism 15
Anne, Queen of Austria 32
Anthony, Susan B. 22
anti-essentialism 87
Antigone 19, 61, 77
Antiquity 27, 32, 61, 67
Arendt, Hannah 19
Aristotle 6, 12, 19, 29, 37, 38, 45, 85
Aspasia 32
Assman, Aleida 9
Astell, Mary 19, 40, 41, 47, 55, 56, 67, 72, 77
Auclert, Hubertine 14

Bauer, Nancy 59
Beauvoir, Simone de 3, 5, 17–22, 32, 34, 35, 37, 38, 42, 50, 51, 53, 59, 68, 77, 79–84, 88–91
Benhabib, Seyla 9, 15, 16, 19
Bentham, Jeremy 74
Berlin, Isaiah 28
binary oppositions 86, 91
biological determinism 89
Blake, William 69
Bocaccio, Giovanni 32, 58, 60, 67
bodies 21, 44, 45, 48, 50, 53, 54, 56, 57, 66, 81, 83, 84, 91
Bonnevaux, Madame de 48, 50

Borde, Constance 22
Bordo, Susan 44
Brontë, Charlotte 36
Brunelleschi, Filippo 36
Burke, Edmund 4
Bush, George W. 15
Butler, Judith 2, 15, 34, 80, 84, 88–91

canon of European intellectual history 2, 10, 92
canon of feminism 20
canon of philosophy 5, 9, 19, 20, 34
canon of Western philosophical thinking 71
Cartesianism *see* Descartes
cartésiennes 48–50
Catherine the Great 56, 67
citizenship 1, 4, 61–77
Cixous, Hélène 84
cogito 35, 45, 46, 59, 62, 80
Colette 19
Condorcet, Marquis de 16, 59, 61, 63–69, 72, 73, 75, 77, 78
Copernicus, Nicolaus 36, 45, 53, 60, 62
Corday, Charlotte 68
Cornelia 32
Coulanges, Mme de 50
Cudworth, Ralph 41
cultural memory 4, 9

David, Jacques-Louis 68
declaration of independence, American 28, 62
Deleuze, Gilles 84

100 Index

Derrida, Jacques 84–86
Descartes, mademoiselle 50
Descartes, Pierre 50
Descartes, René 2, 3, 6, 11–13, 16, 19, 27–29, 34–36, 38, 44–62, 66, 70, 80, 85, 89, 91, 92
Deshoulières, Mme 50
Diderot 65
différance 84
difference 87, 88
Diotima 19, 32, 33, 49
Doeuff, Michele le 19, 23
dualism *see* mind-body dualism
Dupré, mademoiselle 50
d'Hommecour, Mme 50
d'Outresale, Mme 50

écrtiture feminine (female writing) 85, 84
Edict of Nantes 54
education 4, 12, 17, 21, 25, 27, 29, 30, 31, 37, 38, 39, 40, 41, 42, 45, 51, 54, 55, 56, 63, 64, 65, 66, 67, 69, 70, 71, 72, 73, 74, 77
Elisabeth of Bohemia, Princess 48, 50, 56, 57, 91
Elizabeth of England 67
emancipation 14, 16, 49, 83
empiricism 3, 15, 16, 29, 53, 61, 62, 69–71, 73, 74
Enlightenment 4, 9, 11, 24, 26, 29, 48, 49, 51, 58, 59, 61–67, 69–73, 78, 83
epistemology 16, 29, 32, 35, 45, 47, 48, 56, 70, 71, 86
equality 1, 3, 4, 5, 6, 7, 8, 9, 10, 11, 13, 14, 15, 24, 25, 26, 28, 29, 30, 31, 32, 33, 34, 37, 38, 40, 42, 45, 50, 51, 52, 53, 54, 58, 61, 62, 64, 66, 67, 68, 71, 73, 74, 75, 76, 77, 79, 83, 84, 86, 87, 88
equality-feminism 84, 86, 88
equals sign 28
essentialism 87, 91
exemplarity 32
existentialism 21, 22, 80–83, 88

Fairchilds, Cissie 6, 27, 43
fallogo-centrism 85
femininity 5, 15, 17, 18, 37, 44, 59, 77, 82–91

Foucault, Michel 4
Fourier, Charles 14
Fraser, Nancy 15
freedom 13, 21, 29, 49, 54, 63, 64, 68, 69, 70, 73, 75, 76, 81, 83
French Revolution 11, 20, 26, 28, 49, 52, 61–65
Freud, Sigmund 73
Fuselli, Henry 69

Galileo 45
Geistesgeschichte 4
gender 1, 3–7, 10, 12–18, 24, 26, 30–32, 34, 37, 50, 51, 54, 58, 61, 86–92
gender justice 15
gender neutrality 29, 34, 86
genealogical method 4, 8
genealogy 1, 8, 10, 19, 66, 73
Gilligan, Carol 88
Godwin, William 69, 73, 74
Gouges, Olympe de 19, 65, 68, 75
Gournay, Marie de 2, 5, 12, 13, 17–19, 22, 25–27, 29–39, 42, 52, 58, 67, 77, 82, 84, 88
Grignan, Mme de 50
Grouchy, Sophie de 65
Guedreville, Mme de 50
Gypsies 79

Habermas, Jürgen 12
Harding, Sandra 16
Harth, Erica 50, 56
Hartsock, Nancy 16
Haslanger, Sally 14
Hays, Mary 49
Hegel 9, 11, 19, 77, 80
Heidegger 19, 80, 85, 86
Heinämaa, Sara 89, 91
heteronormativity 90
Heterosexuality 89, 90
hierarchy 14, 18, 33, 38, 58, 63, 64, 79, 80, 86, 87, 90
Hobbes, Thomas 26, 28
Holberg, Ludvig 15, 16, 32, 57–60, 67
Holberg Prize 10
homosexuality 68, 91
human rights 13, 62–64, 66, 68, 83
Hume, David 4, 70

Husserl, Edmund 80
Hypatia 32

Ibsen, Henrik 58, 76, 77
Ibsen, Susanna 76
Imlay, Gilbert 69
Index of Forbidden Books 47
innocence 39, 41
Irigaray, Luce 9, 19, 20, 33, 35, 42, 72, 77, 80, 84–88, 91
Israel, Jonathan 24, 29, 62

Jaggar, Alison 14, 15, 26
Jefferson, Thomas 65
Jesuits 47, 66
Jews 79, 82
Johnson, Joseph 23, 69
justice 14, 18, 33, 38, 58, 63, 64, 79, 80, 86, 87, 90

Kant, Immanuel 5, 11, 36, 48, 50, 62, 63, 65
Kelly, Joan 6, 20, 26, 42
Kepler, Johannes 45, 53
Kierkegaard, Søren 80
Klein, Melanie 19
Kristeva, Julia 19, 40, 84
Kristina, Queen of Sweden 50
Kuhn, Thomas 26

Lacan, Jacques 85
Laelia 32
Lanser, Susan S. 36
La Rochefoucauld, François 49
Leibniz, Gottfried Wilhelm 5
Lévinas, Emmanuel 19, 91
liberalism 3, 7, 14, 68, 70, 73, 74, 76
liberty 7, 8, 9, 28, 29, 41, 64, 66, 67, 68, 75, 76
literature and art 79
Lloyd, Genvieve 5, 6, 44, 86
Locke, John 16, 26, 29, 41, 46, 63, 70–72
Longino, Helen 16
Louis XIII 32
Louis XIV 32, 54
Louis XVI 65
Lyotard, Jean-François 84

Malovany-Chevallier, Sheila 22
Marat, Jean-Paul 68

Index 101

marriage 16, 31, 72, 73, 74, 75, 76, 77
Marx, Karl 16, 80
masculinity 15, 44, 45, 84–86, 88–90
Masham, Damaris 41
mathematics 25, 28, 29, 46, 64–66
Melehy, Hassan 36
Merleau-Ponty, Maurice 19, 81
Meun, Jean de 21, 26
Mill, Harriet Taylor 74, 75
Mill, James 74
Mill, John Stuart 6, 16, 50, 61, 72–77, 85
mind-body dualism (Descartes) 44, 45, 54, 56, 57, 60
Mitchell, P.M. 60
modernity 2, 4, 7, 9–14, 24, 27, 35, 45, 59, 67, 92
Moi, Toril 21, 35, 84, 91
Moliére 18
Montaigne, Michel de 16, 25, 30, 31, 34–36, 42, 82
Montesquieu 65
Morrison, Toni 9

natural sciences 29, 46, 47, 53, 63
Nietzsche, Friedrich 4, 8, 9, 11, 19, 80, 85, 86
Nochlin, Linda 20
non-binary gender 89

O'Neill, Eileen 33, 50
Offen, Karen 14, 18
Okin, Susan Moller 6, 7, 10
original sin 47
the 'Other' 2–6, 10, 13–15, 18–22, 24, 26, 28, 32, 34, 35, 40, 44, 46, 49, 52, 53, 55, 57, 58, 63, 68, 70–73, 75, 76, 79, 80, 82–84, 87–92

Paine, Thomas 4, 65, 69
parler femme 85
Parshley, H. M. 22
Pizan, Christine de 13, 19, 21, 26, 30, 32, 37, 38, 58
Plato 6, 19, 30, 32, 33, 41, 45, 58, 61, 85
post-structuralism 2, 80, 84, 85, 90
Poulain de la Barre, François 3, 12, 16, 22, 44, 47, 50–55, 58, 59, 65–67, 73, 77, 83, 90, 91
pregnancy 21, 57, 83

102 Index

Protestantism, protestant theology 38, 40, 51, 62
Pyrrho 33

queer 90
querelle des femmes 15, 21, 26, 27, 30, 34

radical enlightenment 24, 29
Record, Robert 28
religion 38, 40, 51, 62
Renaissance 6, 11, 12, 14, 20, 26, 30, 32, 45, 60, 67
Robespierre 65
Rorty, Richard 4, 9
Rousseau, Jean Jacques 5, 6, 63–65, 71, 72, 74, 77
Rubin, Miri 13

Sablé, Mme de 50
Sablière, Mme de la 50
Salic Laws 36
salons 48–50, 54, 64, 65
Sartre, Jean-Paul 80, 81
Scholasticism 12, 38, 46, 51, 53
Schurman, Anna Maria van 31, 32, 38–40, 50
scientific revolution 26, 63
Scott, Joan 6, 10
Second World War 79, 80
Sen, Amartya 25, 26
Sévigné, Madame de 48, 50
sexual difference 12, 31, 37, 41, 80, 84, 85, 86, 87, 88, 91
sex/gender 51
sexuality 85, 90
sin 27, 39, 43, 47
Skinner, Quentin 7–9
slavery 4, 10, 62, 63, 66, 68, 72, 74, 76
Smith, Adam 4, 65
Smolny Institute 56
society of the friends of truth 68
Socrates 32, 49

Sophocles 61, 77
Spinoza 19, 85
Staël, Mme de 22, 65
standpoint theory
Stuurman, Siep 24, 26, 43, 52
subjectivity 25, 34–36
subjection 73, 74, 75, 76, 77
suffragettes 11

Talleyrand-Périgord, Charles Maurice de 71
Taylor, Charles 3
Themistoclea 32
Theresia, Maria 67
transgender 34
transsexuality 34
transvestitism 89
Trousset, Alexis 27
Tuana, Nancy 14

United Nations Sustainability Goals 26
utalitarianism 61, 74, 76

Vigne, Mademoiselle de la 50
Vins, Mme de 50
Vintges, Karen 21
Voltaire 5, 46, 65
votes for women *see* suffragettes

Wailly, Mademoisele 50
Waldron, Jeremy 25, 29
waves of feminism 1, 11
West, Rebecca 14
Williams, Bernard 25, 47, 66, 67
Wollstonecraft, Fanny 69
Wollstonecraft, Mary 3, 4, 5, 17, 18, 19, 21, 22, 34, 35, 37, 38, 39, 41, 42, 50, 61, 64, 67, 69, 70, 71, 72, 73, 74, 77, 82, 85, 90
woman question 3, 50, 51, 58
Women's Lib 2, 84
Woolf, Virginia 16, 22, 35, 69, 79

Zemon Davies, Natalie 10